NEW PERSPECTIVES ON THE SOUTH

Charles P. Roland, General Editor

The Greening of the South

The Recovery of Land and Forest

THOMAS D. CLARK

THE UNIVERSITY PRESS OF KENTUCKY

Scholarly publisher for the Commonwealth,
serving Bellarmine College, Berea College, Centre
College of Kentucky, Eastern Kentucky University,
The Filson Club, Georgetown College, Kentucky
Historical Society, Kentucky State University,
Morehead State University, Murray State University,
Northern Kentucky University, Transylvania University,
University of Kentucky, University of Louisville,
and Western Kentucky University.

Editorial and Sales Offices: Lexington, Kentucky 40506–0024

Library of Congress Cataloging in Publication Data

Clark, Thomas Dionysius, 1903–
   The greening of the South.

   Bibliography: p.
   Includes index.
   1. Forests and forestry—Southern States—History.
2. Lumbering—Southern States—History.   3. Forest
management—Southern States—History.   4. Deforestation—
Southern States—History.   5. Reforestation—Southern
States—History.   6. Forest conservation—Southern States
—History.   I. Title.
SD144.A15C53   1984   333.75'0975   84-17301
ISBN 0-8131-0305-3

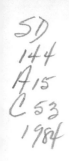

To Elizabeth Turner Clark

Contents

Illustrations follow page 80

Editor's Preface

The region that ultimately became and remains today the South was originally a land of forests. Most of the species of trees that were native to North America flourished in the South. For more than three centuries after the coming of the white man the southern forests gave way to agriculture and to the ravages of the lumber industry. But in the twentieth century, and largely since World War II, southerners and their industries have turned to controlled forestry and tree farming as being among the region's most rewarding enterprises. Thus the recent decades have seen a remarkable new "greening of the South."

Thomas D. Clark is the ideal person to render an account of the greening of the South. As the dean of southern historians today, he brings to this work a vast knowledge of the region's past. He has also lived through, observed, and participated in many of the twentieth-century changes recorded here. Out of this knowledge and experience has come his heartfelt conviction that the land and forests are the South's most enduring resources.

The importance of the topic and the knowledge and insights of the author combine to make this book an important addition to "New Perspectives on the South." The series is designed to give a fresh and comprehensive view of the South's history as seen in the light of the many recent developments in the affairs of the region, the nation, and the world. Each volume attempts to comprise both a synthesis of the best scholarship on the subject and an interpretive analysis derived from the author's own reflections. More than twenty volumes are planned.

CHARLES P. ROLAND

Preface

As a boy growing up in the pine-hardwood forests of central Mississippi about the headwaters of the Pearl River, I was privileged to see the great monarchs that had stood for centuries. The line of virgin trees rolled off in a solid phalanx, with an occasional rosemary pine asserting its dominance over lesser neighbors. These superb "shingle trees" in many cases stood tall in the morning and fell victim to the saw before eventide, leaving a void in the landscape never to be re-filled by such noble patriarchs. Many mill men of that section and time came from Michigan, Illinois, Minnesota, and heaven knows where else to buy timberland and logs, often paying no more than a dollar or two a thousand feet for the latter on the stump. Loggers often cut only up to the the first limb and left behind them in the form of tree "laps" enough wood to build two or three county-seat towns.

Shoulder to shoulder with the great pines, prime swamp oaks and hickories were harvested to be turned into select spoke and hub bolts, houns, axles, and wheel felloes for buggies and wagons, and later into automobile wheels. They were cut to make bridge timbers, cross ties, and lumber for heavy construction. Along with these went the stately old cypresses, which had raised their tousled heads high above sloughs and bayous. Their great boles were hauled away, leaving behind morasses of moccasin-infested rotting tops and stumps to endure for another half a century as grim testimonials to man's assaults on the woods.

In the decades of the frenetic harvest of the South's first forest, shrill mill whistles called men and mules from beds and stables before daybreak to raise towering stacks of lumber and slab and saw-dust mountains. Endless processions of mule- and ox-drawn wagons crawled away from the mills to railway sidings over bottomless clay roads of dust and mud. These were soulless trails of torture that ground men and teams down without mercy or surcease. Then in the end there was a desolate void. The land had been turned into a barrier reef of stumps, its despoilers having "cut out and got out." Behind the departing millmen were the smouldering slab and sawdust piles, the blackened sweep of wanton forest fires left free to consume the last iota of green promise.

There have been few more futile tasks in southern history than that of fighting a roaring woods fire propelled through pine woods by self-generated air currents. In its wake lay the spirit-dampening scene of a tract of timberland left scorched to the roots. Only one other scene is so disheartening and that is of a once-thriving cotton plantation left gullied and wasted by primitive modes of cotton cultivation.

Southerners who lived through the post–World War I economic recession in lumber and cotton prices knew intimately the sting of frustration and vanishing promises. The messages of the forest scientists Gifford Pinchot, Carl Alwin Schenck, and W.W. Ashe, and soil scientist Hugh Bennett were dispatched to self-defeating southerners. A decade earlier far too few people in the South knew about or were concerned with the crusade to secure passage of the Weeks Law, or subsequently its amendments.

In 1921, at the outset of the first postwar depression, southerners faced grim challenges. Occasionally a country editor tried to welcome the future by publishing an edition of his paper on home-fabricated stock. That herald of southern industrial progress, *The Manufacturers Record*, occasionally described an innovative use of wood, and proclaimed it a promise of future prosperity. In the background Dr. Charles H. Herty and other wood products scientists conducted quiet searches for more sophisticated uses of the South's second forest resource. Then came 1930 and the breakthrough in Savannah, in Madison, Wisconsin, and in a kraft mill or two. Herty's impressive speech before southern editors in Asheville, North Carolina, possibly has already had more significant practical impact upon the South than did Henry W. Grady's oratorical proclamation of the "New South." Herty announced the dawning of the age of newsprint manufacture from southern pine pulp. Not even he, however, could foresee how valid his sweeping predictions would become.

As bleak as the Great Depression in the 1930s proved to be for the South, there dawned in the midst of economic disaster rays of hope. The work of the Civilian Conservation Corps was a demonstration of the powers of conservation and reclamation. This national project fell little short of achieving miracles for the South.

Then scientific discoveries showed the way to use southern pine in fine paper manufacture, and pulp, paper, and plywood mills rushed into the region, bringing with them pragmatic managers preaching reforestation and managed timber production. They not only preached but substantiated their messages by purchasing millions of acres of submarginal cotton and scrub forest lands and setting them to growing the South's third, fourth, and, maybe, fifth forests. They established nurseries, isolated superior mother trees, introduced generations of improved seedlings, and their scientists even tinkered with the genetics of hardwoods.

Almost within a generation the land surplus that had borne the gloomy Farm Security Administration down with grief in the New Deal days vanished. Land prices advanced until, in many cases, an acre of good standing timber sold for more than a half section of cutover land in the old Maritime Pine Belt brought in 1925. To date there has been no end of the movement of wood-using industries into the South. They come to the woods, the sun and water, the labor pool, and to short-haul transportation facilities. All of this has brought significant social and economic changes to the region, so deep in places as to create entirely new human relations to the land itself.

Regional historians have too long neglected the subject of the South's forests, of lumbering, and the full impact of the earlier raping of the virgin forests and the abandonment of the land to recover as best it could. There were few conservationists among the first generation of lumbermen—too few in fact who possessed foresight enough to establish a future base for their industry's continued operation. Despite such leaders as Pinchot, Schenck, Ashe, Holmes, Bennett, Hardtner, and a few private corporate landholders, there were not in the South enough militant crusaders to bring about adequate programs of conservation and renewal of forest resources. The new era of conservation and reclamation developed after 1930, and in time achieved dramatic results.

Within the past half-century the South has advanced far enough in its forest history to reveal the fact that the process of timber growth and harvesting has become a seamless social and economic web. One reads the current annual reports of public forest commissions and the wood-using corporations with the sense that despite the great revolution that has occurred since 1930, southern forest industry progress is only at the threshold of a brighter age. Four facts seem to be outlined boldly in the reports: first, forest lands have to be pushed up to much higher levels of production on fewer acres; second, changing American tastes in housing, soft goods, paper, packaging, and industrial materials make increasing demands on mills; third, in no other industry, with the exception of the modern textile mills, has the South been placed in so favored a position as in the fabrication of such a wide variety of commercial goods from wood fibers; and, finally, there appears to be promise of an ever-expanding international demand for southern wood products.

In no manner is this book intended to be a history of the southern lumber industry or of any wood-using industry. These histories have to be undertaken from another perspective. This is, however, an attempt to give some degree of historical perspective to a tremendously important phase of changing resource management in the South.

I have written this book out of personal conviction that the South's land and renewable forest resources are its most durable birthrights. As an active timber producer I personally have gone through most of the procedures of snatching tired old cotton fields away from gullies, broom sage, persimmon bushes, blackberry briars, and sassafras sprouts. I have done practically the same thing with deciduous Appalachian lands.

Before I completed this manuscript I had the good fortune to walk through the pines now growing in Sergeant Tom Crow's reclaimed cotton patch, to cross the Pearl River headwaters swamp where once I saw massive cypress board trees stretching their downy heads up to the sky, and to gaze into an autumn sunset at the dark line of third-generation pines that have sprung up around the spots once occupied by their majestic rosemary ancestors. Too, I have walked through the woods of Appalachia and stumbled over the moss-covered hearthstones of pioneer homes whence former occupants took their departures for Detroit, Hamilton, Indianapolis, Connersville, and every other industrial destination. I am certain that those early soil and forest crusaders like Big Hugh H. Bennett, Charles H. Herty, Charles Mohr, Henry Hardtner, and Walter Damtoft would exult that much of the southern forest land has been set upon the road to become once again the green eden of the primeval past.

A historian using the documentary sources of forest history quickly learns that most of them are in statistical form. One can hardly treat this subject without leaning heavily upon statistics. Lumbering, pulpwood harvesting, and the gathering of all other wood products of necessity have ever been described in quantitative terms. In the myriad reports, surveys, and special treatises their creators have presented almost endless tables and graphs to substantiate descriptive narratives. Throughout this book I have used statistics, but not in tabular form. My intent has been to describe conditions and changes rather than to present broad quantitative measures. I have not attempted to devise tables for the simple reason that it has not seemed a narrative treatment would be well served by doing so. I, nevertheless, am fully conscious that statistics are as vital devices of measurement as are log scales, increment augers, and cords.

Treating a subject so broad as land and forests one incurs heavy indebtedness to a host of individuals. On the home ground I wish to acknowledge the generous assistance of William J. Marshall, Jr., Claire McCann, and Betty Matulionis of the Special Collections Division of the Margaret I. King Library, and of Antoinette P. Powell and Sara M. Bushnell of the Agriculture and Forestry Library of the University of Kentucky. Gene Reynolds, Richard Greene, and Townley Bergman of the Kentucky Department of Forestry supplied the published materials of that department, and allowed me to make a generous selection of photographs from their files. The information staffs of the departments of forestry of North and South Carolina, Georgia, Florida, Alabama, Mississippi, and Louisiana supplied pertinent reports and published materials. I received the same assistance from the informational divisions of the Tennessee Valley Authority, and from the New Orleans and Asheville divisions of the United States Forest Experiment Station. Herbert Finch of the Special Archival Division of Cornell University procured for me some pertinent segments of the Philip C. Wakeley materials. Richard G. Stone of Western Kentucky State University and Clyde Burke of Lexington aided me materially in securing photographs. I am especially indebted to Susan Keig of Chicago for allowing me to read her father's correspondence of the period when he was a student in Carl Alwin Schenck's Biltmore Forestry School. Mr. and Mrs. W.H. Meadowcroft of the Weyerhaeuser Corporation graciously arranged for me to visit the Columbus, Mississippi, plant. Gerald R. Psenka not only accompanied me through the plant, but supplied me with a considerable amount of pertinent material pertaining to its construction and operation and to Weyerhaeuser's operations in Mississippi and Alabama. He also gave me

useful informational suggestions after reading a part of the manuscript. Harold K. Steen of the Forest History Society gave me substantial reading assistance on part of the manuscript. Lastly, my long-
time friend Joseph Clark Robert gave me substantial assistance.

I would be unforgivably negligent if I did not acknowledge that
my wife, Elizabeth Turner Clark, not only supplied patience, but the
opportunity for first-hand experience of reconverting worn-out South
Carolina cotton land to loblolly pine woods.

Such a book as this has of necessity to be an open-ended affair.
Not all the data are ever in, nor can they all be compressed into a
modest volume. Enough of the record is available, however, to establish the fact that generous chapters of the South's economic and social
history have been profoundly influenced by the fortunes of the region's forests.

1. Land of Tall Timber

As a youth I rode many times with my family past a worn and eroded cotton patch in central Mississippi. My mother said the land was snatched away from the pines a second time by our neighbor Tom Crow. As a sergeant in the 15th Mississippi Regiment he was badly wounded in the Battle of Shiloh Church. Three years later he lost a leg in the great military debacle at Franklin, Tennessee. In the end Sergeant Crow, like Margaret Mitchell's Will Benteen, hobbled home on a wooden peg leg he had fashioned from a black-gum bolt. For the rest of his life he whittled and scraped this peg leg into a more refined shape. Back home in the Mississippi hills he began all over the herculean task he had undertaken when he followed the cotton and land rush out from South Carolina to the Choctaw Indian territory.

Scarcely three decades before Tom Crow and his neighbors had rushed headlong into war, the land on which they had settled was home to the forest-dwelling Choctaws. Nearby on a knoll overlooking the Dancing Rabbit Creek, and beneath a towering cathedralesque arch of virgin pines, shrewd and unscrupulous Jacksonian treaty commissioners, led by the wily General John Eaton, had negotiated the infamous Dancing Rabbit Treaty of cession, which technically ended Indian occupation of that portion of the great primeval southern forest and opened the land to an inrush of yeoman cotton farmers.

All across the South returning Confederate veterans warred as zealously against the stubborn regrowth of old-field pines as they fought on battlefields from Shiloh to Appomattox. Slowly they pushed back the perimeters of their hillside fields and pastures, sweating through interminable seasons of axe-wielding to clear the land, rolling logs and burning brush heaps. From the upper reaches of Chesapeake Bay to the eastern rim of Texas they attacked the woods, all but destroying the virginal chain of nature and planting in the region a new agrarian economy. These veterans, like their forebears were steeped in the traditional practices of the American frontier, wasteful of both forest and land resources. From the outset of the great southern migration into the western forest reaches of the lower South, they busied themselves laying low virgin stands of pine, cedar, cypress, and swamp-grown hardwoods.

Anglo-American pioneers in the Old Southwest during the first half of the nineteenth century enjoyed the distinct privilege of walking beneath the vaulted canopy of virgin trees that had grown for 150 to 500 years on the site. Early visitors to the region left accounts of wandering on horseback and in wagons through the forest, where vast areas were practically free of underbrush. Longleaf pines and bayou-rooted cypress pushed their heads up to heights of 150 feet, atop boles that measured at the butts from thirty to seventy inches in diameter, many extending up a hundred feet to the first limbs. Most of these primeval giants were already thriving sawlog trees when the English began planting settlements along the Atlantic coast.

It is difficult for present-day southerners to visualize an area of approximately 400,000 square miles lying silently and awesomely in virgin woods. Of the five major regions of the United States the South was most generously blessed with forest trees of commercial importance. Its coastal areas and highlands produced three major pine types. The Appalachian Highlands, including the Blue Ridge and Great Smokies, were covered with one of the richest varieties of deciduous trees to be found on the globe. It was not by accident that the Indian civilization of these areas was arboreal; long before the coming of the later tribes of recorded history, paleolithic men wandered across this wilderness, strewing campsites and burial and ceremonial mounds, and sowing the soil with arrow points and stone instruments.

The longleaf pine belt extended in a sweeping crescent band around the coastal South from Virginia to East Texas, embodying roughly 230,000 square miles of territory, or 147 million acres of timber cover. This area comprised one of the noblest forest stands of virgin timber east of the Rocky Mountains. The tree, known botanically as *Pinus palustris*, yielded some of the finest softwood lumber and timber products in American economic history. Its seasonal growth rings were tight, its face patterns were regular and attractive, the wood possessed great strength under stress, and it was remarkably resistant to wear and weather. This stately pine yielded lumber and forest products for a great variety of uses: ship timbers, roofing shingles, pitch, tar, and turpentine.

In the longleaf pine barrens of the Old Southwest several chapters of regional, national, and international history were shaped. The sprawling conifer forest was criss-crossed by the hunting and war trails of Indians, who developed impressive social and political organizations beneath its protective cover. Then a highly competitive pastoral and agrarian society moved rapidly into the region and forced an abrupt reversal of land uses and destinies. Just as the pine belt had sheltered a distinctive native culture it was now to nurture a white and black Anglo-American slave culture. This region was to develop distinct folk characteristics and to create a regional type of American frontiersman who responded to environmental conditions and local political and economic issues within a severely parochial context.

The outer Maritime Pine Belt hovered around the Atlantic and Gulf coasts, with frequent undulations marking coastal bays and marshes. This region was dissected by an intricate system of rivers and lateral streams bearing such memorable names as James, Albemarle, Cape Fear, Waccimaw, Pee Dee, Altamaha, Escambia, Chattahoochee, Tombigbee, Black Warrior, Choctawhatchie, Leaf, and Pearl. These all poured their floods through primeval forests, cutting paths of ingress and egress. Unfortunately these watery paths would open the forest to timber exploiters, who from earliest times of European invasions set about to rape the magnificent virgin pine stand.

Bordering the sprawling coastal pine belt was the tremendously important secondary one of pines mixed with hardwoods at the higher elevations. The most important of the upland pines were the shortleaf, *Pinus echinata*, and its humbler cousin *Pinus taeda* or loblolly. Among the premium quality hardwoods were the oaks, tulip poplar, ash, black walnut, chestnut, hickory, black cherry, linden, and maples. Like their aristocratic relative the longleaf pine in the coastal region, the shortleaf species grew to impressive age, diameter, and height in the upland forest. Many a southern dwelling was to be roofed over by boards and shingles cut from patriarchal shortleaf and loblolly "rosemary" trees. From the standpoint of long-range timber harvesting this belt was even more impressive than was the one along the coast. All these highland pines had distinct advantages over the longleaf types in being able to perpetuate themselves under even the most adverse circumstances and without depending upon man for assistance.

No doubt the loblolly pine was God's atonement to the South for southerners' wanton abuse of their land and natural resources. Like the mule, the scrawny striped sinewy steer, the razorback hog, the goat, and the hound dog, the loblolly pine was capable of raising its head afresh, no matter how harshly abused. The tree can restore itself and even thrive on man's wasted acres. It can do this despite the redness of the soil and the depth of the gullies; it always struggles back. By its tenacity to survive and spread under its own power, the loblolly pine has defied the follies of man with success so long as it has not been seared by wild fires.

The South in nature, as in geography and history, is by no means a unified region. Its cover is highly diversified, made so by soil types, climate, rainfall, and topography. From the beginning of the time when greening of the earth occurred, southern swamplands grew cypress, gum, hickory, oak, and cedar in prodigious volume and quality. Along the murky sloughs, in flooded brakes, and across the higher flood planes, these hardwoods pushed their spreading branches up shoulder to shoulder with the bordering pine horizons. Rolling back in seemingly endless waves of dark green, the ridges and river valleys of the Appalachian South were covered with billions of feet of saw timber of prime quality. Indian hunters, warriors, and wandering herds of wild grazing animals mauled paths through the ever darkening shadows of the virgin woods. In time the backwoods long hunters wandered beyond the western fringes of settlements to explore this endless forest. Among them came such characters as Daniel Boone, Michael Holsteiner, Simon Kenton, the Skaggs, the McAfee brothers, and all the rest. They traveled, hunted, and camped beneath natural cathedrals of yellow poplar and its giant neighbors in the coves, benches, and tablelands of the highland South. But consistently this great forest was regarded only as a worrisome barrier to human advance and security.

In all the literature dealing with the old western and southwestern frontiers there is scarcely a hint of conservative management of resources, not even of the land itself. Southern border heroes were wasteful exploiters of the eden they so joyfully invaded. They came to the great forests with a pastoral gleam in their eyes that portended the destruction of the woods to recreate the old-world concept of the happy cotter on the land. In the history of the frontier these folk have been projected as heroes who persevered in snatching the land from the Indians and nature itself by the expenditure of blood and sweat. Building cabins, clearing land, splitting rails, rolling logs, and firing brush heaps—these were basic accomplishments to the newly arrived settlers.

No historian or statistician can ever establish more than a generalized estimate of the ultimate cost to the South of the wanton destruction of its virgin timber resources. This was done largely in the name of progress and civilization in remarkably few years. Earlier census reports of southern timber harvesting were too poorly devised to be even remotely dependable. At best, early statistical reports of southern timber harvesting must be considered as no more than indicators. Enumerators listed the number of sawmills and cooperage operations, but clearly the results reflected their careless procedures in gathering even the meagerest information.

No contemporary economist or experienced timberman or forester was on hand to go behind the official counts to explain the void created by the cutting of centuries-old black walnut trees, of the felling of a whole stand of ancient swamp cypress in which only the choice butt cuts of logs were taken. In the harvesting of virgin swamp and Appalachian hardwoods, pioneer loggers before 1850 left behind kings' ransoms in the less desirable cuts beyond the first limbs. Again it is much easier to document the waste left in the woods than to discover any sense of obligation on the part of anybody to future southerners to replant specimen trees that had demonstrated adaptations to particular sites. To the average antebellum southerner, ignorant woods-dwelling cracker, or even agricultural essayist, the science of silviculture would have seemed highly impractical if not utterly foolish. Even so erudite an editor as James D.B. DeBow largely ignored the subject of the forests in his popular regional economic journal.

Paradoxically the Old South, with superb stands of hardwood immediately at hand, imported from abroad and the North much of its furniture, farm implements, vehicles, and wood-based machines. Even so, the history of the early exploitation and exportation of the southern cypress stand by both Latin and American loggers combined the unforgivable sins of waste and economic shortsightedness. This was a slow-growing tree, which only with careful selective cutting could survive as a continuing source of lumber and heavy construction timbers. In a more positive manner the harvest of timber from the southern lowlands, however wasteful, challenged American industrial ingenuity in providing transportation and milling. Within the scope of a couple of generations prior to 1870 much of the southern cypress and lowland cedar resources were laid to waste, much of it never to be regenerated to anything approaching the virginal state.

It is still possible in secluded coves in parts of Appalachia to see the outlines of walnut and chestnut stumps that stretch the imagination to conceive of the massive trunks that once sprang up from the woodland floor. Many of these decaying shells linger as grim monuments to the ravages of man and his wanton fires. Settlers' animals also were vandals of the first order. The long-snouted, seed- and root-devouring range hog was a demon of destruction, especially in the deciduous woods. Whenever hogs ranged in numbers in deciduous forests they reduced materially the capability of the woods to renew themselves.

In Appalachia, mountaineers armed with ax and torch laid low the woodlands in the ignorant and irrepressible belief that the timber stand was inexhaustible. They constructed their crude houses by the most extravagant use of wood that could have been imagined. Log houses with their thick-hewn walls reflected the skill and ingenuity of the craftsmen who raised them, but the score marks of the broadax on their sides were tell-tales of the waste on the woodland frontier of the basic regional resource, which under proper management would have assured a continuing economic well-being. To frontiersmen moving onto the broad stretch of virgin land, the woods seemed to hold little promise; this fact, however, in no way mitigated the enormous waste of timber in clearing land, building cabins, barns, fences, and other farm structures.

This attitude lingered in the South throughout the nineteenth century. In the latter decades, a capital city could have been constructed from timber utterly wasted in the building of rail fences to keep scrawny free-ranging cattle and hogs out of growing crops. In the enactment of range fence laws in the closing decades of the last century, southern legislatures gave little or no thought to the tremendous economic impact this use of timber would have upon their states' basic natural wealth. Over a span of a century and a half the South must have sacrificed many hundred million feet of prime logs, which were split into rails only to rot in hillside fences or burn in forest fires. If the value of the livestock they enclosed had been compared with the ultimate timber deficit the loss would have staggered even the most ignorant farmer. Winston J. Davie, Kentucky Commissioner of Agriculture, reported to his constituents in 1879: "There are in Kentucky (in round numbers) 125,000 farms, which will average about 600 rods of fencing to the farm. This will aggregate 75,000,000 rods, 150,000,000 of single panel worm fencing. To build this amount of fencing will take nearly 2,000,000,000 split rails, and not less than 70,000,000 of good rail trees. To keep this immense amount of fencing in annual repair would require a yearly consumption of 280,000,000 of rails and the destruction of not less than 10,000,000 of timber trees. The money cost, or value in labor, of this enormous quantity of fencing, is not less than $75,000,000, and the annual cost of keeping it in repairs is not less than $10,000,000 in the entire state." The commissioner may have been a bit dazzled by his calculations, but he described the general situation in eleven southern states, a fact which is ignored in forestry publications.

Added to this shameless waste of timber was the incalcuable drain of annual woods firings. Historians of the Civil War and Reconstruction have written voluminously about wartime property losses from fire. Two horrendous examples that continue to excite scholars are Atlanta and Columbia. Thus far no one seems to have established a firm estimate of dollar losses suffered in the destruction of parts of these cities that can be equated with modern monetary worth. But there can be little doubt that losses all across the forested South from fires set by wartime actions were considerably greater than those in the cities. Fires were set willfully or accidentally in battles, by untended campfires, by marching troops, and by nonmilitary vandals and arsonists. For the first time in southern history the wood-burning, spark-belching locomotive was brought into fairly common use, a marvel of technological progress but a monster of destruction. In its wake across broad stretches of forest lands fires raged for almost three-quarters of a century. This menace seems to have been tolerated first as a consequence of war, then as a blaze of industrial progress.

Southern losses from wild fires that raged across the region after 1861 were seldom if ever listed as one of the significant costs of war. Added to losses directly attributable to military activities were those resulting from southern folk myth and ignorance. Annually, torchbearers deliberately set the woods afire to "green the grass," burn up snakes, kill chiggers, ticks, and mosquitoes, or to drive out game. From 1820 down into the mid-twentieth century the South was befogged by the smoke and haze of woods-destroying wild fires. So commonplace were these conflagrations at the turn of the century that country newspapers scarcely took notice of them. Local editors and other community leaders seem not to have been deeply disturbed by this wholesale destruction of timber, nor did they seem to be aware that fire cut off at least a generation of forest growth.

For the antebellum period DeBow's *Review* makes little if any mention of forest fires. The same is true of the contemporary agricultural journals. Occasionally a traveler through the South commented in his journal that he had seen the woods on fire. Southerners themselves shrugged off fire losses and the regularity of their seasonal occurrence. As a matter of fact, the haze of Indian summers and the pungent smell of burning duff was thought to have a nostalgic appeal.

As in nearly every aspect of the southern forest economy, losses from forest fires can only be loosely estimated. With one exception, no statistical information on this is available. In the gathering of data for publication of the Tenth United States Census, in 1880, a pioneering attempt was made to inventory the nation's forest resources and to assess the rate of harvest. There was a precedent; a revealing survey of the forest resources of the United States had been published in 1876 as part of the United States Commissioner of Agriculture's *Annual Report*. Although the report was for the year 1875, the forest data may have been gathered in the census of 1870.

In his introduction to the more extensive forestry volume in the Tenth Census Report, Charles Sprague Sargent, arboriculturist of the Arnold Arboretum, wrote:

> As we shall see further on in this report the most important part of our forest resource is in the coniferous supplies, among these especially the pines, the white of the North and the yellow pine of the South. These latter covering vast areas, not less than 100,000,000 acres, furnish now, and still more in the future, the most important staples of our lumber industry, and the white pines are giving out. There still is the possibility of treating the uncut balance of these pineries in such a manner as to secure their continued productiveness.

This was a seasoned and conservative naturalist speaking; it was an impossible dream for the times in America. Though the overwhelming majority of southerners lived in or near their region's forests, few of maybe none had any real knowledge of silviculture beyond the most elementary notions of botanical classifications. They had only limited knowledge of the processes of forest renewal and conservation and seemed to have little interest in these areas. They and their immediate forebears had from the beginning of Anglo-American civilization engaged the forest in ceaseless battle to clear and keep cleared enough land on which to plant corn, cotton, rice, and sugar cane, and even to establish graveyards. Fire was a merciless weapon in speeding the performance of these tasks. The historically romanticized log rollings, cabin and barn raisings, and land clearings accounted for the destruction of millions of acres of virgin forest lands, much of it land that should never have been denuded of tree cover in the first place and quickly became eroded submarginal fields. What axmen and men armed with handsticks failed to accomplish, the torch completed by the destruction of woods in the burning log piles.

Almost as a matter of course, log and brush-heap burnings got out of hand and fires roared through neighboring woods destroying mould, seeds, and seedlings. Injury and destruction of mature timber was clearly visible to even the dullest and most indifferent; what was not readily visible even to intelligent observers was the long-range damage, not only in the form of immediate destruction of the necessary elements of reproduction but to the land in the form of heavy erosion, a fact that has plagued southern history through all the generations since Europeans began to clear the forests of the South.

In no part of the southern forested area was it more necessary to maintain the extremely delicate balance of nature than in the Maritime Pine Belt. The longleaf pine required undisturbed primeval conditions for self-renewal. This tree bore a viable seed crop only every seven or eight years, and conditions on the ground had to be favorable to the seed's penetrating into mineral earth and sprouting. Upon reading Charles Mohr's extensive inventory of the southern pine resource, B.E. Fernow commented that the longleaf pine "eminently needs light. Loblolly and shortleaf, better fitted for warfare with other species, will do much better in their respective habitat to recuperate, except in mixed forest. . . . Considering that the timber on which we now rely and on which we base our standards comes from trees usually from one hundred and fifty to two hundred years old, and that none of these pines makes respectable timber in less than sixty to one hundred and twenty-five years, the necessity of timely attention to their renewal is further emphasized." This warning was ignored for more than half a century.

For the first time the enumerators for the Tenth United States Census reported estimates of fire losses in the nation's forests. During the census year fires raged over more than 10 million acres of American woodlands. This has to be accepted as little more than a rough guess, and a conservative one at that. In the deflated monetary terms of 1880, the loss to the South was estimated to be over $7 million from the burning of 5.3 million acres. It is impossible to conclude from the census whether fire losses for the calendar year 1880 were average or not. If, however, this was a representative year, then in a century and a half the South would have suffered the staggering loss from woods burnings of more than $12 billion, a sum that makes General Sherman's firemen appear to have been little more destructive than lightning bugs on a pleasant summer evening.

Already by the 1880s concerned observers like Charles Mohr, M.A. and A.H. Curtiss, Edward Kidder, W.C. Norwood, and B.E. Fernow had come to realize the long-range meanings of the wanton destruction of the southern forests. The fire losses recurred year after year, compounding losses not only in the butt scarring and permanent injuries to mature trees, but in completely destroying the life-sustaining duff of the ancient forest floor. If these losses had been compounded semiannually at six per cent, the ultimate monetary costs to the South might have been triple or quadruple the income from cotton and the other southern staple crops.

The blame for fire losses must be placed at the door of every southerner, but the poorest strata of southern society, the tenant farmers, share tenants, and backwoods dwellers, were the worst offenders. They fired the land about them, opening the soil to wholesale erosion, a fact eloquently established in Hugh Bennett's startling reports on southern soil conditions in 1912, but even more graphically in the lingering gullies themselves. It was a blessing indeed that the persistent shortleaf and loblolly pines had the capability of withstanding three-quarters of a century in which much of the human population of the South plowed itself almost irredeemably into land exhaustion and agrarian poverty.

Luckily for future southern forest historians, the southern forest estimate that appeared in the Tenth Census was placed in the charge of Charles Mohr of Mobile, a botanist and practical forester who at the time perhaps had the soundest overview of regional forest resources of any southerner. His unusually perceptive report was the first overall inventory of the maritime stand of pines; all other appraisals had been made in the most general terms by casual observers or by self-serving local timber buyers. The Mohr report, on which a good part of the census text of 1880 that applied to the South was based, indicated there were 230,000 square miles of timbered lands, an area almost six times the size of Kentucky. These acres, he said, were highly adapted to forest growth. Of the area he estimated that 90 million acres then grew 170 billion board feet of lumber. He thought an additional 47 million acres of southern swamp and ridgelands were covered with hardwoods. Mohr demonstrated less firsthand information about this tremendously important hardwood resource in both the swampy and highland South. He made no estimate of the quality or quantity of the standing deciduous timber.

Generally the southern hardwood forests exhibited radically different characteristics from the neighboring pine belt, and the swamp-grown trees varied in many ways from their ridgeland cousins. Within an area of 102,000 square miles, or 18.4 million acres, the Eleventh Census of 1890 estimated that southern hardwood forests contained 12 billion board feet of construction and furniture grade lumber. This deciduous growth, swamp and highland, had tremendous powers of recovery by both seeding and sprouting, provided the woods were protected against the ravenous razorback hog, wild fires, and other destructive forces. From this area both national and international markets were to be supplied with large quantities of hardwood products during two centuries of American lumbering.

Aside from producing trees of many varieties and of fabulous sizes and qualities, the southern hardwood forests made an indelible impression upon the folkways and life of people who dwelt beneath their canopies. These woods produced an almost endless variety of fruit-bearing shrubs, of berries, and nuts. Some of the giant black walnut, chestnut, and hickory trees yielded enormous annual crops of edible mast, and the heavy oak cover littered the forest floor with layers of acorns to provide food for wild game and domestic hogs. Matting the ground as low-growing underbrush were shrubs compatible with the heavy overstory. Most of these flowered, bore berries, and had aromatic roots that could be converted into specifics for the folk treatment of the ills of man. These shrubs gave the spring-time southern woods their color and romantic attraction.

All the southern hardwood cover helped in some way not only to sustain a varied wildlife population, but to help shape the mores of human dwellers. Folk of the deciduous timber region colored their homespun cloths with natural vegetable dyes, regulated their blood and bowels with natural teas, and even eased the pains of childbirth and death with herbal concoctions gathered from the floor of the woods. In no other portion of the nation was human life so thoroughly integrated with natural forest resources as in the hardwood areas of the South.

The way of life in the southern woods had a pronounced impact on human personality, the woes of life, and social attitudes. This fact was brilliantly reflected in a regional genre literature and in the views of travelers who chanced to cross the backwoods South. A.B. Longstreet in *Georgia Scenes*, Joseph Glover Baldwin in *Flush Times in Alabama*, and George Washington Harris in the *Sut Lovingood Yards* described an emerging Anglo-American way of southern life, which on the one hand reduced the more sophisticated social ways and institutions of the coastal colonies to the barest natural limits, and on the other replaced the old way of life of the forest-dwelling southern Indians.

Two local-color authors of a later age, John Fox, Jr., and Horace Kephart, updated the earlier descriptions of backwoods life. Fox, the Kentuckian, wrote of hill country life at a time when commercialization of the region's forest and mineral resources was in the initial stages, the era when mountaineers first discovered they could cut and raft the giant hardwood trees downriver to outside markets and receive modest payment in cash for their labors and risk of life and limb. This was also an era when every major stream valley in the hills spawned personal vendettas. Throughout the writings of John Fox, Jr., there is a recurring awareness of the insulative virgin forest, which screened out the influences of the world beyond the ridges.

To the east in the Great Smokies, and at a somewhat later date, the librarian-bibliographer Horace Kephart sought social escape among the western North Carolina and eastern Tennessee mountains. He was more sociologically aware of human adeptations to the environment of the rugged highland reaches of these hills. He sensed perceptively the influence of the towering forest upon the economic, social, and moral lives of the population trapped in a cul de sac of

American civilization. The mountain ranges closed in horizons geographically, and the woods inverted them physically and psychologically. Kephart's people lived out their existences in an age of wood in which most of their needs were served by the forest and its fruitful floor. In more recent years, the popular *Foxfire* books have recalled the simple skills and homely means by which the Appalachian highlanders adapted their lives to the hardwood belt.

In the expanding post–Civil War machine age the lives of southerners became entangled in America's insatiable demand for lumber and forest products. Mountain trails were widened into log and lumber roads, rivers became gorged channels of log rafts, tramline spur railways were pushed up the forbidding slopes of the mountains, and trunk railroads were built up river valleys. The wooded horizons were gapped as ancient chestnut, oak, tulip poplar, and mountain white ash patriarchs fell victims to ax and saw; the old first forest was doomed to almost immediate disappearance.

Lumbermen in the decades 1880-1920 thought only in terms of production as measured in board feet of lumber, and let the future take care of its problems of forest renewal and timber conservation. Maybe after all Sergeant Tom Crow would have gained economically if he had been content to sit under the shade of a pine and let its progeny take full possession of his cotton patch. In time he was to lose this, his second cause. It was a harsh affront to the old southern yeoman farmers who struggled so gallantly to fight back the pines from their fields that in time the invader would come to have far greater economic significance for the South than all the cotton and other crops they could produce. In the latter half of the twentieth century Tom Crow's pitifully worn and eroded Mississippi acres came to be worth more money than he earned in his entire lifetime of gruelling labor, hobbling up and down cotton rows on a wooden leg.

2. Carpetbaggers of the Woods

During the blustery winter of 1888 the ambitious young Chicago author William H. Harrison looked out upon the harsh Great Lakes surroundings and dreamed of escape. He wanted to depopulate the city and get rich by doing so. His thoughts dwelt upon the South where, he said in his book *How to Get Rich in the South*, one could raise everything from goats to castor beans while basking in eternal sunshine. "The South," he said, "possesses greater natural wealth than all the balance of the Union." There were other and more down-to-earth adventurers who cast their nets in the southern woodlands to ensnare fortunes. In these closing years of the nineteenth century northern lumbermen were turning to the southern forests to continue their heedless exploitation of the American timber resource. "The supply of timber is inexhaustible," said Harrison, "and the list contains the names of all the trees known to the North and many that are unknown, and of great value, and is being bought in large tracts by [northern] lumbermen."

Southerners too seemed to believe the region's timber resource was inexhaustible, and that the land beneath the forest was of minimal value. Blinded by ancient folk attitudes, much of the southern population felt the heavy stand of timber was actually a barrier to the spread of civilization. Pine-belt backwoodsmen regarded a good forest as one lying in log and brush heaps ready for the application of the torch.

In the Old Southwest, huge tracts of public lands could be acquired at only a fraction of their actual worth, even by contemporary monetary standards. Some public lands could still be had for the traditional price of a dollar and a quarter an acre. Other lands, held by private owners, could be procured by the simple process of paying the delinquent taxes. An ignorant seller of an invaluable tract of long-leaf pine at only a fractional amount of its true worth was said to have taunted his "victim" saying, "Now you have made your bargain—live with it."

Although the South was not lacking in numbers of sawmills (5,573 in 1880) their operational capacities were modest, and to date they had done little more than nibble around the edges of the virgin forests that bordered the rivers, bays, and the newly built railroads. For example, there were still standing in the older states of North and South Carolina in 1880 an estimated 10 billion board feet of longleaf and loblolly pines and hill-country hardwoods. During that year Carolina lumbermen cut only 175 million board feet, maybe even less than the annual growth of the forests.

Deeper into the crescent of pine forest in Florida, Georgia, Alabama, Mississippi, Louisiana, Arkansas, and East Texas the woods remained untouched by lumbermen. Settlers had largely bypassed the heavily pine-studded lands because of the arduous labor required to clear them, and because their thin siliceous soil was too poor to sustain even a meager subsistence agriculture. Cotton farmers and other settlers had brought scarcely more than a quarter of the area of Mississippi under cultivation and public use. There remained large swampy sections too wet for either profitable timber growth or farming. Charles Mohr, in his famous *Bulletin 13*, estimated that in 1879 there remained in Mississippi 9,000 square miles of mature longleaf pine, and that each of the other coastal states carried at least as much growing stock.

Since the opening of the gulf coastal lands to public sales in 1810 the results had often been desultory and disappointing to federal and later to state land agents. In most of the wooded South in 1870 it was possible for speculators and millmen to manipulate the land laws to acquire large tracts of pine and hardwood lands at ridiculously minimal cash outlay. Post–Civil War homestead restrictions to eighty acres failed miserably to achieve their objectives. Negro freedmen found it difficult to start anew on cleared and reasonably fallow ground; they were unequipped both physically and financially to bring under cultivation eighty acres of densely forested pinelands. They and their white neighbors stuck to older agricultural areas, devising at the same time a system of share-tenancy to continue the traditional mode of staple-crop farming, and left the forested areas to be exploited later, largely by outsiders.

Historians of the South have slighted the bitter congressional fight that ensued over attempts to revise the Southern Homestead Law of 1866. In 1876, the law was revised to permit unrestricted cash entry, and the door to the southern timberland was thrust wide open. Land speculators of every stripe rushed into the region in search of virgin tracts of timber to lay low. The southern largess made available is reflected in the fact that 47.7 million acres of federal lands in the five gulf states remained unsold at the outbreak of the Civil War. After 1880 speculators and lumbermen gobbled up millions of acres of virgin timberlands at the standard century-old price of $1.25 an acre. By this date southern public lands were coming into heavy demand both for their timber cover and underlying coal seams and iron ore. Within a decade after the repeal of the Southern Homestead Law approximately 6 million acres of federal holdings in the five gulf states had been sold. In addition there were sales of large blocks of state lands.

The latter-day timberland carpetbaggers came largely from New York, Michigan, Indiana, Illinois, and even from Kansas. There were also southern scalawags who battened purses on the opportunities of the moment. Some examples of the unusually large purchasers of Louisiana lands were N.B. Bradley, Bay City, Michigan, 111,188 acres; F.H. Head, Chicago, 109,645; J.B. Watkins, Douglas County, Kansas, 145,335 acres. Northern purchasers between 1880 and 1888 secured deeds to well over a million acres of Louisiana lands alone. Across the Mississippi line, buyers acquired almost a million acres of pinelands, and in Alabama another half-million acres. In all approximately 6 million acres of federal lands were preempted within half a decade. In 1888 and 1889 Congress moved to restrict purchases, but the cream of the southern public lands, state and federal, had been skimmed by 1890.

Long before the latter date the Federal Government had learned that policing public southern piney woods was an all but impossible task. Federal and state governments were unable to end the wholesale thievery of timber. When logger and sawmill vandals were apprehended by United States marshalls it proved virtually impossible to secure court convictions, largely because local sentiment favored the lumbermen, who offered jobs. Again, no official estimate could be made as to the volume of stolen logs that drifted down southern rivers and bayous to sawmills whose managers asked no embarrassing questions, or how many of the operators themselves cleared enough profits from the thievery to remain in the business.

On the eve of the inrush of the big mills most of the lower southern coastal longleaf pine forest was a silviculturist's dream. The broad sweep of gulf coastal pinelands was studded with stems that reached seventy feet or more of merchantable boles. Charles Mohr, in his vivid description of the Mississippi longleaf forest in 1880, wrote:

> The almost unbroken pine forest covering the upper tier of counties between the Pearl and Pascagoula rivers toward the northern confines of the pine region, are still practically intact. The wealth of these forests has yet found no outlet to the markets of the world. Thinly settled, they are still largely the property of the government, but in view of the speedily increasing demand for lumber and the profits derived from the lumber business, such a condition of affairs must soon come to an end. It can be safely asserted that by far the largest part of the timber, felled in the Abolochito region is taken from government lands. There can be question of this when it is considered how insignificantly small is the area of land which has been legally entered by private persons along that stream. The necessity of adopting proper measures to protect the timber wealth of the public domain from depredations of such enormous extent forces itself upon the most casual observer, while to one who looks closer at the consequences of the continuance of the existing state of affairs the urgency becomes appallingly apparent. The ever-increasing consumption of timber at the mills on the Pearl River, of which one alone can cut 100,000 feet of lumber a day, will prove a powerful stimulus to people who, since the development of the lumber business in these regions, have almost completely abandoned their former agricultural and pastoral pursuits and now depend entirely for their support upon cutting pine logs, to supply this enormous demand at the expense of the public's property.

The ink was hardly dry on Mohr's classic report before the longleaf pine region of the South was being penetrated by land-grabbing railroads and logging railways and tramlines. In order to solve their transportation problems most southern states had made large grants of land to railroad companies. Within immediate reach of the gulf coastal pinelands, the opening of the vital mile-long Ship Island Canal through the shell-encrusted barrier reef to reach navigable waters gave a boost to the earlier southern lumber trade. Also the opening of the passway from the coastal lakes to the Mississippi provided a direct shipping route from the Pearl River mills through the port of New Orleans. There was much heavier pressure, however, for the development of transportation lines to penetrate deeper into the sprawling southern forest than rivers and coastal waterways could accommodate.

Before the Civil War the South had little more than outlined a system of local and trunk line railroads. Most important of the main connecting lines were the Memphis and Charleston, the Georgia system, the Mobile and Ohio, and the several links of independently operated roads that formed the New Orleans to Cairo connection. In the post–Civil War years local roads such as the New Orleans and Northeastern through the Pearl River country and the network of internal Alabama, Georgia, and Florida local branch lines were merged into the Louisville and Nashville, the Southern, and the Seaboard systems, opening for southern lumbermen much more effective access to the domestic market for lumber. Later the Gulf, Mobile, and Northern was extended northward from the Gulf of Mexico to central Tennessee, penetrating enroute the central Mississippi pine belt. All of the southern railroads were lined with sawmill villages, which supplied both freight and passenger income. In fact sawmills and planing mills were more prominent in this corridor of the South than were cotton gins, and they produced a far greater volume of heavy freight.

Internally the hauling of logs and lumber over mud-and-sand southern back country roads was an all but impossible challenge. It would be difficult to exaggerate the grinding physical demands on men and animals in the hauling of logs and lumber overland in the South, 1870-1920. The horrible suffering of mules and oxen from gnawing collar and yoke galls alone constituted a traumatic chapter in the inhumanity of early southern lumbering. Laborers, black and white, were subjected to the same harsh demands as were the galled and bleeding animals they whipped into and out of mudholes. This repulsive fact was absent from both statistical tables of production and written accounts of the industry. Seldom if ever did local journalists take note of it and certainly none of the commercial trade journals commented on this aspect of lumbering operations. It can be sensed, however, in the report of an Illinois sawmill operator in central Mississippi, who boasted that his philosophy of running his business was "kill a mule buy anothern, kill a nigger hire anothern."

The larger companies alleviated somewhat this living horror. They developed systems of privately operated secondary railroads that took up where rivers and bayous left off. The southern log railroad was an anomaly in American transportation history. Roadbeds, bridges, and tracks were temporary in nature. Even locomotives and rolling stock were of specialized and uncomplicated construction. Yet these temporary "mudlines" greatly facilitated removal of timber from broad reaches of southern pinelands. Traces of these rights-of-way have been obliterated by passage of time; even bridges and grades have been leveled by erosion and decay.

Southern river and bayou raftsmen, a small army of "John Henrys" and "Paul Bunyans," steered contrary flotillas down treacherous floodtide streams as skillfully as river pilots maneuvered packet boats. No southern author, however, has fully extolled their adventures, no grand festivals have commemorated their heroics in chopping, sawing, rolling, lifting, burling, drinking, and loving. Their diet would have caused college-bred dietitians to run and hide, and their swearing was subject enough to rouse many an angry camp-meeting evangelist to the highest pitch of revilement. Southern log-rafters were masters of all the above feats. Historians have been cotton-blinded, seeing mostly staple agriculture, slavery, sectional politics, and "wasted" southern society.

Equally neglected were those artisans who served so arduously the ultimate challenges of lumbering at the stump level. Just as raftsmen drifted almost unnoted into oblivion, so did those experts who swung eight-foot crosscut saws with the grace of ballerinas vanish from the scene. In this age of the power saw and motorized shears it is hard to recall the deftness and speed with which earlier sawyers dragged forth saw-length worms of "dust" with every swing of the blade. Few if any axmen in American frontier history handled that humble instrument with such dexterity and heft as did southern woodsmen. Behind the tables of rising lumber production were always woodsmasters who initiated the process of leveling trees. They were almost unerring in throwing towering pines where they wanted them to fall, in measuring by eye the lengths of logs, keeping eyes peeled for falling "widow-makers," and watching constantly for leg crushers that rolled around underfoot.

From stump to mill other experts handled logs. These were mule and ox drivers who snaked and loaded logs while stumbling about in the brush, stirring up furious yellowjackets nesting in stump holes, and shouting profanity by word and verse vociferously enough to unsettle all southern religious creation. It took brawn and patience to yoke eight pairs of stubborn oxen, or to catch up and harness an equal number of fractious mules, and then to creep along beside a creaking eight-wheel log wagon day in and day out. All of this for meager cash reward, and an even more meager living.

Labor in the mills was no less gruelling than in the woods. Man was driven by machines. Steam-propelled saws were soulless task-masters, more so than were cottonfield overseers. To run through saws from 40,000 to 150,000 board feet of lumber a day required working at a constantly driving pace. With the introduction of im-proved saws, the "shotgun" carriages, and "nigger head" log turners, off-bearers and lumber stackers were kept hustling. From whistle to whistle of eleven- and twelve-hour days, laborers in both big and little mills worked as if all civilization were threatened with collapse if the South did not deliver its share of American lumber.

By no means was the southern pine industry monopolized by lumbermen. Since earliest English colonization on the Atlantic Coast extractors of turpentine and tar products had operated an important industry. With the expansion of the southern frontier, turpentine dis-tillers advanced into the Old Southwest. Wherever pine trees yielded rich returns in resin the distillers pitched their camps and bled or-chards. Turpentining was perhaps the most primitive form of com-mercial forest exploitation. Inherent in it was the serious wounding if not total destruction of many of the younger trees in the Maritime Pine Belt.

Following the War of 1812 the naval stores industry was centered largely in North Carolina. Resins and gums from this state's forest supplied both domestic and foreign ship builders, rope winders, and paint manufacturers. This specialized forest product, however, had economic significance only in localized areas of the South, and was at first confined almost altogether within the longleaf pine belt.

As southern population advanced inland, so did the turpentine industry.

Boxing pine trees in the gathering of resin did not always spoil them for other uses, but it seriously lowered the grade and desirability of lumber sawed from their butts. Young trees twelve to eighteen inches in diameter were hacked, and for three years the scars or boxes were moved upward to induce further bleeding. In the third year the tree's circulatory system and resin quality were badly weakened. Turpentining left behind forests that were resin-permeated and highly flammable. They burned with the fury of gaseous torches.

Turpentine harvesters were notoriously careless with fire, and almost as a matter of course wild fires roared through orchards and adjoining forests with seasonal regularity. Many of the fires resulted from the turpentiners' practice of burning accumulated duff from around the bases of trees in order to establish better footings. Often the orchard fires were left to burn out of control and destroy more timber than the resin harvest was worth.

North Carolina in 1880 was the largest resin-gum producer among the seven major southern pine states. In that year its producers gathered and distilled 6.3 million gallons of turpentine and over 650,000 barrels of tar; the entire South produced approximately $8 million worth of naval stores. Wilmington was the center of this trade, and A.H. Van Bokelen of that city wrote:

> The production of naval stores is carried on in a wasteful, extravagant manner, and the net profits derived from the business are entirely out of proportion to the damage which it inflicts upon the forests of the country; the injury is enormous. Lumber made from trees worked for turpentine is of inferior quality, although it is probably less injured than has generally been supposed. Comparatively few trees, however, once boxed are manufactured into lumber. It is estimated that 20 per cent of them, weakened by deep gashes inflicted upon their trunks, sooner or later are blown down and ruined; fires, too, every year destroy vast areas of the turpentine orchards, in spite of the care taken by operators to prevent their spread.

For the southern pine belt as a whole the enormity of the loss by wasteful turpentine harvest was measured in terms of the stunted growth and reduced quality of thousands of square miles of young and growing pines. The abandoned orchards fell ready victims to fire, recurring storms, insect damage, and internal decay. Blazing or boxing killed some trees outright, but most were left ghostly shafts of lighter wood to become flaming torches of forest destruction. In some places the "fat" wood and stumps were gathered for use in home fireplaces or for fuel to heat industrial boilers. More of it was piled into tar kilns from which the remaining resin was extracted by application of intense heat to become "rope-makers' tar."

Partly as a result of turpentine orchard fires North Carolina in 1880 suffered a loss of $357,980 from the burning of over half a million acres. Although this was less than a dollar an acre, the cumulative annual losses were staggering, amounting to approximately three and a half million dollars. Between 1860 and 1880 the loss in this state from annual woods fires was a sum that possibly equaled that spent by the state on its university.

In time Georgia, Florida, Alabama, and Mississippi pine woodlands rang to the staccatto chopping of turpentine axes. Hacking trees, emptying resin boxes, and scraping coagulated gum from old blazes required constant attention. The scoring was done with specially designed tools, and had to be repeated for a period of two and a half years before the operation ceased to be profitable. This was exhausting and often degrading work in which all the predictable dangers of the woods were involved. Laborers who operated the stills fared no better than the hacking and gathering crews. The distilling plants were crude affairs surrounded by barrels of resin, and the process of extracting turpentine was hot, sticky, and always odoriferous, with workers being constantly exposed to fumes. If life in the logging camps was drab, that in the turpentine orchards reached an even more primitive level. Workers were mostly blacks "recruited" from chain gangs, convict camps, and anywhere else they could be found. Some were kidnapped outright; others were forced into peonage because they were unable to repay usurious and intolerable debts. Wages paid turpentine laborers were low, hours were long, the torment of insects almost unbearable, and general living conditions were minimal at best. "Turpentine recruiters" were busy in many parts of the South in their efforts to keep the pinewoods supplied with workers. This sordid chapter in southern industrial history is eloquently described by Pete Daniels in *The Shadow of Slavery, Peonage in the South 1901-1969*.

Modernization, which came much earlier to the sawmill industry, was largely unknown in the turpentine woods until well into this century. The first advance was the result of the experiments of Charles H. Herty, a chemist at the University of North Carolina. During the decade 1900-1910, he perfected the Herty cup or box, which was much more efficient than the one in use since colonial days.

Herty's breakthrough led others to work at modernizing the turpentine industry. After 1910 some recognizable changes occurred in the processes of gathering and distilling wood extracts. Use of chemicals greatly facilitated the extraction of resins from pine and other woods. The old-fashioned rosin-smeared still with its barrel yards has now largely disappeared from the southern pine forests, and gone with it in the past quarter century are the camps populated by the most miserable of southern laborers.

In present methods of harvesting, hacked turpentine trees are stimulated to yield a more continuous and abundant flow of gum by generous applications of sulphuric acid. Important gums extracted from other trees exceed those extracted from bleeding pine trees. The old industry with its inhumane system of peonage labor is remembered only as a dark chapter of southern history. This industry produced no heroic entrepreneurs, inspired no tales of magnificient accomplishments, invited no minstrel singer to pass on its traditions in soulful ballads, and no one to mourn its demise. Pine trees still bleed, but their wounding and treatment are done with greater skill and scientific knowledge. Too, the industry has experienced stifling competition from a considerable volume of synthetics, changes in paint bases, and from a revolution in marine construction and repair.

Historically, lumbermen and turpentiners had about the same relationship in the southern pinewoods as did cattlemen and sheep herders on the western ranges. Fundamentally the two industries were incompatible. In the long run the turpentiner was unable to compete successfully with the lumberman, who destroyed potential orchards all across the Maritime Pine Belt. After 1910 the lumbering industry greatly outstripped all other exploiters of the southern woodlands.

In rapidly changing times, world economic conditions far removed from the sandy reaches of the Maritime Pine Belt and from the hardwood coves of Appalachia placed an onerous levy upon southern forest resources. The gathering storm that resulted in World War I was to have an immense bearing on the southern lumber industry. Europeans, and the Germans in particular, purchased large volumes of lumber between 1910 and 1914. Rivers in the upper South ran flush with log rafts during spring and fall "tides." Kentucky log rafts before the big mills at Cattlettsburg, Valley View, Ford, West Irvine, the Panbowl, and Paducah were tied up along streams for miles. Log tramways and railroads pushed their tentacles deeper into virginal stands of hardwoods. Mountaintops earlier considered inaccessible were now scored with thousands of log dumps, in which timber could be tumbled down cliffsides to lower levels. Ox and mule teams scarred hillsides with snake roads, which became permanent documentation on the coves themselves of the raping of the first forest.

In the years of frantic harvest, 1880-1914, West Virginia, Kentucky, and Tennessee loggers harvested 3.557 billion board feet of timber by the turn of the century, and in 1914 they produced an annual cut of 2.549 billion feet. Production during the intervening years was equally high. By a conservative estimate these states yielded in all 45.76 billion board feet of lumber in a decade and a half. This meant stripping mountains and coves of the major stand of virgin timber, so that by 1928 the annual harvest had dropped to 1.252 billion board feet. By the latter date most of the large mills such as those at Paducah, Nashville, Charleston, Valley View, Ford, Cattlettsburg, Harriman, Middlesboro, and West Irvine in Kentucky and Tennessee had largely cut out their stands, leaving behind them millions of monumental stumps to memorialize temporarily what had once been a noble forest. The enormous white oak stand across the Big Sandy in West Virginia was also leveled, leaving hundreds of square miles of barren mountaintops and abandoned sawmill sites. Along the Tug Fork River where Hatfields and McCoys had warred, most of the stand was stripped of its timber. In the North Fork Kentucky River country the great Mowbray-Robinson Timber and Land Company had cut out its stand by 1921. Their mills stood idle and abandoned, railroad trackage fell into disrepair and decay, logging equipment rusted at the spot where it loaded the last logs, and the sawmill village at Quicksand became another seedy mountain community. Behind the Mowbray-Robinson operation lumbermen left mountainsides and coves stripped of their immediate economic promise. In order to relieve themselves of tax and management responsibilities officials of this company deeded their cutover lands, and later, the mineral rights, to the University of Kentucky for future administration and use.

The Mowbray-Robinson cession to the University of Kentucky was an exception. Elsewhere in the South, most of the cutover land that passed from lumber company hands reverted to states and counties for delinquent taxes, and local governments and public institutions suffered from the reduction in tax bases. All across the southern hardwood and pine belts, thousands of square miles of dreary denuded lands went begging for purchasers and users. In 1917 these offered only the bleakest prospects of eventual productive recovery. This was particularly true in the longleaf Maritime Pine Belt.

Most visible of all the southern cutover areas was the longleaf belt, where the stand of virgin pines was of common age and size, so that nearly every tree was harvested. Too, the topography of the region was fairly level, and logging operations opened broad vistas of destruction and desolation; in contrast the paths of loggers in the hardwood stands of Appalachia had a relatively low public visibility. What loggers started, careless later management completed. Too few mother trees were left to reseed the area, even if the longleaf pine could have done so naturally under prevailing conditions.

Eras of southern timber and wood products harvests shade into one another, definable only by the level of stand depletion. The years of World War I, however, may well be considered a watershed in the history of the forest industry in the South. The shocking and wanton harvest during these years was a sobering experience, the memory of which lingers in any historical consideration of the South's forest resource.

3. Nesting Birds and Wooden Ships

From the outset of the big mill operations in the South lumbermen sought to open and supply the European and British markets for lumber and specialized wood products. Many of the companies, like the hardwood producers Burt and Brabbs of Ford, Kentucky, maintained foreign sales and market survey offices. With the expansion of the foreign trade after 1908, it is reasonable to believe lumbermen would have leveled most of the South's stand of virgin timber in supplying the demands of foreign and domestic consumers. After 1914, however, the harvest and wastage of southern timber was hastened. American involvement in World War I generated an insatiable demand for lumber.

When German buyers were shut out of the southern lumber market, British and allied purchasers immediately took their place. Subsequently German submarine warfare and surface naval campaigning sank enough southern lumber in the North Atlantic to floor much of that ocean. The heavier the losses the more frantic grew demands for southern forest products. The impassioned cry of Lloyd George that Britain needed "ships, more ships, and still more ships," meant that southern lumbermen would be asked to produce astronomical amounts of heavy dimensional timbers and plankings. When the United States entered the war enormous pressures were exerted on southern lumber mills to step up production, for the government had to construct from the ground up industrial plants, shipyards, warehouses, ships, office buildings, and military training camps. Thirty-nine of the latter were located across the nation, with such heavily populated ones as Fort Jackson, Camp Shelby, Beauregard, Pike, Croft, and Forts Knox and Bragg in the South.

In May 1917 an estimate was published that it would require 600 board feet of lumber per man to house a million-man army. The war was to be a heavily woods-oriented one, creating urgent demands for forest products to manufacture everything from dummy rifle forms to be carried by raw recruits to filtering substances for use in gas masks. No demand, however, was more dramatic or potentially wasteful than that for specialized timbers to be used in the construction of wooden cargo ships.

In April 1917 the National Lumber Manufacturer's Association, meeting in Chicago, pledged to "answer every demand made upon our patriotism in the spirit of our forefathers in the industry." Lumbermen proffered the output of their mills to the government, having in mind at the moment needs to construct semipermanent quarters for the new "universal army" and the building of a thousand ships for the navy and the merchant marine. Whatever the mainspring of their loyalty, the millmen recognized that the war generated a bonanza for their industry. Government marine specialists estimated that each of the proposed wooden ships would require from one to one and a quarter million board feet of prime lumber, most of which was to be of a selected specialized quality standard.

No mill in the South in 1917, no matter its size or diversification, was equipped to supply all the timbers needed to construct a seaworthy ship. S.H. McLaughlin, president of the Waussau Southern Lumber Company of Laurel, Mississippi, said in May 1917 that every stick of timber sawed to build ships had to be cut to the precise specifications for a particular vessel. "Under these circumstances," he said, "you can readily see that no mill can carry a stock of this class of material."

Characteristic of such frantic planning amidst so many uncertainties was a vagueness about timber needs. Even the official decision to build wooden ships was delayed until late spring 1917. In May of that year further fuel was added to the argument when General George Washington Goethals, of Panama Canal fame, and briefly chairman of the United States Board of the Emergency Fleet Corporation, spoke at an American Iron and Steel industry banquet and seemed to say he thought wooden ships impractical. In his gruff and tactless manner he ridiculed the idea by saying that birds were still nesting in trees from which southern lumbermen proposed to cut ship timbers. Before his brief chairmanship of the corporation ended, General Goethals came to respect the sting of southern wrath.

Answering General Goethals and all the other bureaucratic doubting Thomases of the United States Shipping Board, William B. Stillwell, secretary-treasurer of the Southern Pine Company of Georgia, gave assurance that southern sawmills could supply the necessary timbers and dimensional lumber if the government would diversify its bids in such a manner as to permit submission of complete bids by several operators. Approval for wooden ship construction was given June 4, 1917, and Atlantic and gulf coastal shipyard owners were instructed to build merhant marine vessels on a fixed-price basis.

General Goethals was prompted to make his much-publicized remark in support of riveters and iron workers who, he hoped, would be drawn away from non-war-related industry to help build steel ships. Too, he assumed it would take an inordinate amount of time to season lumber for ship building. In normal dry building construction such seasoning is imperative, but in shipbuilding pine timbers—especially those cut from longleaf stock—being impregnated with water-resistant resin, do not require seasoning. Under any circumstances wood submerged in water would immediately reabsorb a good amount of moisture. For the first time in southern forest history, abandoned turpentine orchards became sources of lumber of commerical value.

The first contract for wooden cargo ship construction was awarded the New York firm of Edward T. Terry and Henry L. Brittain Company. They promised to build twenty composite vessels at their Moss Point, Mississippi, plant. Soon contracts were awarded to other shipyards, some of them hastily organized to take advantage of wartime business. Yards were located in Hampton Roads, Savannah, Brunswick, Tampa, Pensacola, Mobile, Pascagoula, Jacksonville, Houston, Gulfport, and Port Aransas. By January, 1918, the Shipping Board had contracted for $400 million worth of ships in the South. The region's shipyards became magnets drawing carpenters and other laborers from all across the South. Never before had there been such an inrush of craftsmen.

Ship launchings became as frequent as southern barbecues. From Baltimore to Port Aransas, graceful wooden vessels slipped down the ways, each containing approximately a million and a quarter board feet of selected lumber. The Emergency Fleet Corporation in April, 1918, made a special occasion of the launching of the 3500-ton *Nacagdoches*, named by Mrs. Woodrow Wilson. This was the first vessel constructed in the Houston Shipyard. Before this event occurred, however, the Emergency Fleet Corporation, in true bureaucratic fashion, decided that the light wooden ships were too small to permit economical operation.

In that year there were plans under way to launch a hundred vessels on the 4th of July. A silver loving cup was designed to be awarded the shipyard foreman who built the best ship. In Jacksonville alone seven ships were launched, and as many new keels were laid. A premature cheer went up that this activity meant "continued ship-building for the South Atlantic for many years." Before its echo died away it was evident that the approaching end of the war would bring cessation of the industry.

Never was war's waste more dramatically revealed in America and the South than in the feverish building of wooden ships that, after all, the Emergency Fleet Corporation concluded, were too light for efficient cargo handling. Behind the shipyards the sawmills produced billions of board feet of top grade lumber, so much in fact that General Goethals' birds were hard pressed to find branches in the cutover sahara in which to anchor their nests. War's end in November 1918 doomed southern wooden shipbuilding, and for years thereafter Atlantic and gulf coastal inlets and bays were anchorages for the graceful wooden ghosts that never put to sea. In terms of southern forest resources this program resulted in a disastrous depletion of timber that would require more than half a century to reestablish even a token renewal. It had taken at least a century and a half for the virgin stock to mature.

The most reckless sawmill operator in the South in 1915 could detect certain signs that the end of the region's first forest of virgin timber was rapidly approaching. In the coastal pinelands and Appalachian hardwood ridges the woods-robber era was ending, leaving implanted on much of the South a deep stamp of shame and impoverishment. With singleminded purpose, sawmill operators had flooded billions of board feet of lumber onto domestic and foreign markets without regard to the future.

The end of the great sawmill era in the South coincided roughly with the cessation of World War I. Wartime demands were so pressing and lumbermen so firmly committed to the production of a staggering amount of lumber that end results were obscured. By 1925 southern forest land history had come full circle. The sawmills desolated millions of acres that originally had been unattractive to early settler-buyers, and were now even less desirable. Most of this land was a blackened fire-scorched world, dominated by millions of stumps.

Scattered scarred pine saplings and brushy hummocks remained lonely testaments of the past, and even these were subjected to further desecration by raging wildfires that burned unchecked.

In the summer of 1917, in the midst of feverish war activity, southern lumbermen and farmers met in New Orleans on August 2, to organize the Southern Cutover Land Conference. Delegates sought answers to the nagging problem of restoring barren timberlands to some form of production. Proposals were made to entice northern and foreign immigrants to colonize, farm, and reforest the abandoned lands. Present were representatives from the United States and state departments of agriculture. George M. Rommel of the Bureau of Animal Industry was present and actively engaged in the discussions. There was agreement that soil surveys should be undertaken to determine the adaptability of cutover lands to grazing and growing of specialized field crops. Plans were made for a national and international advertising campaign to attract settlers. An immediate search was to be made for a quickly maturing type of tree to replace the depleted longleaf pine stand. One suggestion was the introduction of Chinese tung oil trees, which would produce an annual harvest of oilbearing nuts, a project of which the Illinois Central Railroad was a major promoter. In some areas papershell pecan orchards were established, and considerable acreage was planted to strawberries. These successful introductions, however, used only a small portion of the cutover acreage of the southern pine belt.

Though reforestation was mentioned in the conference call, the actual discussion in New Orleans emphasized the use of cutover land for pastures and the growing of crops. J. Lewis Thompson of Houston, Texas, was elected president, Clements Ucker was made vice president, and J.E. Rhodes was appointed secretary-manager. In the long and complex program delegates confronted two problems, for neither of which they had an immediate solution. First was the fact that the cutover belt was known to be infested with Texas fever ticks; until this menace could be eradicated the promotion of cattle raising was an impractical proposal. Second, the land was covered with millions of solidly anchored "fat" pine stumps, which would resist decay for an undetermined interval of time. Deep tap roots made pulling them an arduous if not impossible task. No poorly capitalized farmer could afford the cost of pulling four hundred to a thousand stumps per acre just to clear second- or third-rate land.

A difficulty of converting pinelands to pasturage and agricultural uses was demonstrated by the Houlton Lumber Company in Uneed-us, Louisiana. W.L. Houlton had cut out a white pine stand in Wisconsin and then allowed the land to revert to the state. When his mill had cut out its Louisiana stand he vowed not to repeat the Wisconsin mistake. He set out to convert 500 acres of his holdings to farmlands. His first problem was getting rid of the stumps his loggers had left behind. He attempted to pull them and dig them out of the ground. Neither plan worked satisfactorily. He then split the stumps with charges of dynamite and set them on fire. Houlton did establish a farm operation with fine barns and open pastures, but the cost was far greater than the average southern farmer could afford in reclaiming cutover land, even if the land were free. Houlton estimated in 1918 that his farming reserve was covered with over 4 million stumps.

Carlton J. Corliss wrote in *Main Line of Mid-America* that "In Mississippi a few years ago (1920) forest products accounted for about 40 per cent of the tonnage and about 18 per cent of the freight revenue originated on the Illinois Central in that state. Proportionately, traffic in these commodities has declined in recent years, owing, in part at least, to the fact that millions of acres of excellent forest land, unsuited for other purposes, has [sic] been stripped of its timber in both Louisiana and Mississippi and is presently a total loss to its owners as well as to the state." The railroad promoted a reforestation program.

By no means did the entire South suffer the cutover land dilemma of the Maritime Pine Belt. In areas where slash (*palustris*), shortleaf (*echinata*), and loblolly (*taeda*) thrived, natural seeding was sufficient to compete somewhat with range hogs, forest fires, and stifling undergrowth. A saving grace of these trees was that fruitful mother trees scattered seed widely on air currents. In areas of the inland pine belt, where in 1920 it seemed forests were permanently devastated, old-field pines made remarkable recovery within two decades. But though nature was prodigal in seed production, it would take intelligent forest management of the reseeding and renewal processes to promote the maturing of the South's second pine forest.

In Appalachia most of the cutover lands had only to be protected from man's wasteful practices to promote the restocking of the region with quality second-growth trees. Too, the forest had to be protected from the ravages of domestic animals, especially the hog. Almost miraculously there remained in the soil an abundance of seed, which—if not destroyed—awaited the opportunity to sprout and grow in the open sunlight. Unhappily all across the South "peckerwood" sawmill operators were unwilling to allow this second-growth timber to stand long enough to mature into top-quality lumber. Like jackals they followed the big mills, slashing down everything that would make a two-by-four.

Few of the operators of the larger mills seem to have made plans to continue the operation of their businesses by protecting their timber stands. They made little if any investment in forest research, gave no material support to reforestation, preserved few or no mother trees, practiced no selective cutting, and made no attempts to preserve vital ground mould. To say that the average sawmill operator in the late nineteenth- and early twentieth-century South was ignorant of the science of tree growth and silviculture would not be uncharitable. They were largely oblivious to the capability of the woodlands to restore themselves under common-sense forest management.

Despite the noise and hustle of the big southern sawmills of the earlier part of this century, they were wasteful and inefficient in their operations. New machines introduced were designed to facilitate production, not to conserve resources. Many of the new machines, like the logging locomotives and the steam skidders, were actually destroyers of the forest. Never in American economic history was an industry more prodigal in handling precious raw materials than were the southern lumber mills. Day by day veritable mountains of sawdust accumulated about the mills. Old-style heavily swaged saws cut quarter-inch kerfs with every line sawn through a log. In a twenty-foot log yielding ten two-by-ten-inch planks there was a wastage of approximately twenty-one board feet of lumber. Often the last surviving evidence of a sawmill site was the sawdust pile, which like Mount Vesuvius smouldered for years as fire burned at its heart.

Slabs, although some were burned in boiler furnaces, represented a greater waste than did sawdust. Farmers hauled them away for fire and stovewood, to build slabsided fences, or to lay causewaying over mud roads; most, however, were burned. A third source of waste occurred in the dome-shaped tower that caught and burned shavings from planers.

In 1906, in designing what company officials claimed would be the largest sawmill in the world at Bogalusa, the Great Southern Lumber Company estimated that it could operate on that site for another quarter century before its timber stand would be exhausted. Provisions were made to utilize all of the log except the bark. To do this the Louisiana Fibre Board Company was organized, and by 1915 this mill was producing fifty tons of coarse kraft paper daily. In order to continue in business the company developed a private rail and highway transportation system, encouraged private landowners to plant shortleaf and slash pines to reforest the cutover areas, and gave more care to its own harvesting procedures.

The Bogalusa experiment (which will be discussed more fully later) was an early exception to the practices and attitudes of the vast majority of southern sawmill operators, as to both utilization of scrap materials and reforestation. Generally, hardbitten "practical" lumbermen scoffed at the idea of central gathering and utilization of waste products. They contended, perhaps rightly, that they could not afford the necessary equipment to process the waste material. Before 1920, by conservative estimate, an amount of timber equal to the growth on 20 million acres went up in smoke and flames, or rotted and burned in sawdust, shavings, and slabs.

By the end of World War I the day of the old-line "cut-out-and-get-out" lumberman was rapidly drawing to a close. In 1917 Stanley F. Horn, of the *Southern Lumberman*, sensed this fact. He wrote of the "timber robber" that "like the carpet-baggers, he was out for what he could take away with him, and took no thought of the communities in which he operated. A new spirit is dawning in the South, and the lumberman at the present and future looks beyond the day when the last log is cut and the mill dismantled."

It took a major economic crisis to help initiate new regional attitudes toward use of the South's submarginal land and forest resources. Simultaneously with the exhaustion of the virgin timber stands, Hugh Bennett, the pioneering soils specialist with the United States Department of Agriculture was publishing the surveys of southern soils. In 1911 the surveyors assigned to Fairfield County, South Carolina, reported:

> Many steep hillsides have been cleared and planted to cotton and corn, and these have become so badly gullied and washed as to prevent tillage. Such fields are to be found in all sections of the county and are now grown up to old field pines. Not only these hillside fields, but many of more gentle slope, have been allowed to reach the same condition. Besides the loss in farm acreage due to the abandonment of these upland areas much bottomland has been made worthless by a covering of

sand washed down from the cleared uplands. It is believed
that at present as large an acreage lies idle and abandoned
from this cause as is actually under cultivation.

This description was to be repeated for counties all across the South.
Hugh Bennett's 1914 predictions of serious damage to regional soils
because of erosion were borne out even to the dullest observer by
1930.

Rapid depletion of southern lands by repetitive and primitive farm
operations and the removal of the region's forest cover reached their
nadir of regional impoverishment almost simultaneously in the 1920s.
But in its highly publicized report on economic conditions in the South,
1934-1938, the National Emergency Council devoted its attention largely
to agrarian shortcominds, scarcely touching on the subject of reforestation. Using the report of the Fifteenth Census (1930), Howard W.
Odum in the preparation of his provocative *Southern Regions* did only
little better in analyzing the subject of forest products consumption
and tree growth. The decade covered by the Fifteenth Census was
indeed a traditional one in southern forest management.

There may be some justification, in the face of past wantonness, for
modest nostalgia at the passing of the great sawmills. In the period
of their presence in the South they introduced new ways of life, ways
that contrasted sharply with those of the traditional agrarian civilization. In some ways the mills acted as social and economic safety
valves by drawing away from cotton tenancy surplus laborers who
had no alternative source of employment. In the heavily forested parts
of the South, the regional aroma abruptly shifted from magnolias and
cape jessamine to freshly sawed lumber, sweating mounds of sawdust, and smouldering slab pits.

Southern laborers, black and white, were quickly transformed from
field hands to brash sawmill men. In the latter role they differed distinctly from the wielders of the hoe and the plow, as distinctly as if
they had never been near the farm. Most of them, however, traded
peonage to the sharecropper landlord and the country furnishing store
for peonage to the lumber company commissary. They found mill
bosses, bookkeepers, commissary clerks, and timekeepers more diligent in keeping track of indebtedness than were the casual farm cred-
itors.

Sawmilling exerted its particular kind of hardening influence upon the men who labored in woods and mills. They came to reflect the harsh ends of an industry that seemed destined for oblivion and left more than 150 million acres of forest lands an economic shambles with a sea of stumps as grim monuments to the demise of a precious natural resource. With the end of the sawmill era in the pinewoods the emigration arteries to East St. Louis, Chicago, and Indianapolis ran flush with laborers in search of employment in northwestern industries. Those along the Atlantic coast moved northward to Washington, Baltimore, Philadelphia, and New York City, and their shabby sawmill-camp shanty homes melted into the ground along with the sawdust and slab piles.

Of fundamental historical importance in the South, the end of the sawmill era brought the actual closing of the frontier itself. It would now require a new and scientifically oriented sense of economic and sociological direction to recast large areas of the once heavily timbered South with the new tools of management, resource renewal, and industrial organization. The vast land, once possessed by four major Indian tribes in the Old Southwest, then invaded by somewhat peripatetic Anglo-American cattle and hog drovers and subsequently by yeoman farmers, would now require conservationists, trained foresters, capitalists, firefighters, and new and sophisticated industries. As wasteful and sinful as the first southern timber harvest was, it possibly was the only way to effect this revolution in management and the awakening of a sense that one generation of southerners is indebted to the next.

The ending of the old era, whatever its shortcomings, must not be passed over without the observation that the great mills produced an immense volume of lumber that may never again be equalled in quality and beauty.

4. Dawning of the Age of Scientific Forestry

During the most intensive years of the exploitation of the first American forests there were not more than a dozen Americans who had any working knowledge of the science of silviculture or sound economic management of timberlands. Along with the rest of the country the South remained burdened with the frontier myth of the inexhaustibility of natural resources, a myth carried over into and abetted by the laissez faire pillaging of the first forest. In the half century from 1870 to 1920, there emerged a trace of alarm if not guilt on the part of some sawmill operators and concerned citizens. This feeling, however, was too remote to move legislators, private landowners, and lumbermen to initiate effective changes.

In the Congress self-aggrandizing politicians continued to battle over public land policies as they affected special interests, and gave no discernible heed to conservation of natural resources as a broad public policy. During the tumultuous years of the Grant administration the nation lacked both scientific information concerning the extent of its forest resource and the trained talent to organize and promulgate a constructive program to conserve at least a part of its seemingly inexhaustible woodlands. Actually there was not in the United States in the 1870s a scientifically trained forester, an academic course in the science, or much if any public sentiment to remedy the situation.

Earlier in American history a sizable group of botanists and naturalists, native and foreign, prowled the woods to discover, classify, and describe native fauna in both scientific catalogues and travel accounts. The Michauxs, father and son, for instance, performed noble yeoman service as classical botanists, but their writings indicate only peripheral concern with the social and economic impact of plants upon the human population. The same thing was largely true of John and William Bartram, the New Harmony botanists and scientists, Sir Charles Lyell, and many others.

The emerging colleges and universities of the latter period, and especially the land grant institutions, largely ignored in their formative years the field of forestry as a legitimate area of scientific instruction and investigation. In the era 1865-1920, the United States was almost entirely dependent upon Germany, France and Switzerland for the training of foresters and advanced scientific knowledge of silviculture. Through centuries of wanton exploitation of timber stands and the ravages of recurring wars, Britain and Europe had come dangerously close in the decades after 1850 to exhausting their woodlands. As a result of the crisis Germany, France, and Switzerland were foremost in development of a forestry discipline, public awareness of the need for conservation, creation of a workable public management policy, and the scientific training of foresters. Advances made in forest sciences abroad were to have a distinct impact in the United States.

Between 1870 and 1890 a series of events and personalities influenced American attitudes toward conservation of natural resources, and in time had important influence on the economic future of the South.

In 1872, the nation was shocked by the devastating Peshitago forest fire in Wisconsin. This conflagration destroyed hundreds of thousands of acres of timber and took the lives of 1,500 people. It demonstrated that human lives and the fate of natural resources were often suspended on the same slender thread of chance. The following year (1873) James Arnold of Massachussetts established a fund to support a professorship of silviculture in Harvard University. The Arnold Arboretum, at Jamaica Plain near Boston, through subsequent studies under the direction of Charles S. Sargent introduced the first scientific information about the physical properties of trees, the nature of their growth, and a wide range of taxonomic data.

In the centennial year of American independence the American Association for the Advancement of Science prevailed upon the United States Congress to authorize a thorough analysis of the nation's forest resources. This resulted in the appointment by the United States Commissioner of Agriculture of Franklin Benjamin Hough as forestry agent. Hough was a Martinsburg, New York, native, who spent his professional life in Lowville. A graduate in medicine who had seen extensive military service in the Union Army, he had served as superintendent of the 1870 census for New York. He had also made several reports on the American forests, including a memorial to Congress to enact a forestry law. In his new position in the Federal agricultural commission, Hough was instructed to make a survey of forest resources.

With the publication of the annual report of the commissioner of agriculture in 1876 and subsequent surveys by Hough, Charles Sprague Sargent, and later Bernhard Eduard Fernow, southerners had available to them for the first time in their history a reasonably comprehensive notion of their land and its forest cover. County by county the commissioner of agriculture's report compared farm lands with the adjoining forested areas, using graphic charts and statistical tables to indicate the contrasts. All the southern states in that year, with the exceptions of Virginia and West Texas, were represented as being heavily primeval. In counties like Hancock, Greene, and Jackson in Mississippi, and St. Tammany, Washington, and St. Bernard parishes in Louisiana, 85 percent of the land was under forest cover. In the Atlantic coastal states of North and South Carolina and Georgia the percentage of forest in comparison with farming areas ran almost as high.

The forestry section of the Tenth United States Census (1880) was under the imaginative direction of Charles Sprague Sargent, director of the Arnold Arboretum. For southerners the materials contained in this section were indeed enlightening. As remarkable, however, as these surveys and reports were it is doubtful that many southerners ever saw them or knew of their existence.

Prior to his appointment as forestry agent in the Department or (Commission) of Agriculture, Franklin Benjamin Hough had already published an impressive amount of material on forest resources, and by 1877 he had ready his first agency report. Before his retirement as forestry agent in 1885, he assisted in the preparation of three more annual reports. Though not a trained forester in the European sense, Hough may well be regarded as the father of analytical forestry in the United States. Because of his outstanding service as forestry agent he was made, in 1881, head of the newly created Forestry Division of the Department of Agriculture. In time this division was to become an effective arm of the United States Government in devising and promoting legislation pertaining to American forest resources.

Coincidental with the publication of the first forestry report in

1876 there arrived in this country a German immigrant who down to 1903 exerted a strong personal influence on national economy and life. Bernhard Eduard Fernow, a native of Inowrazlaw in the Province of Posen, Prussia, and trained in the German forest service, upon his arrival in the United States became manager of the Cooper-Hewitt and Company forest lands in Pennsylvania. In 1882 he was the personal force behind the organization of the first American Forestry Congress. In later years this organization helped to develop conservation policies, stimulate special legislation, and promote the training of foresters and the creation of national forest preserves.

Fernow wrote an impressive introduction to Charles Theodore Mohr's survey of the southern pinelands in the Tenth Census. In 1886 he was appointed chief of the Forestry Division of the Department of Agriculture, and in 1898 became professor of forestry in Cornell University, where he was one of the pioneers in establishing the profession of forester as a proper field for academic training. In 1891 Fernow prepared the first reserve law, which laid the foundation for the creation of the federal forest preserve. Personally the Prussian was said to be stubborn, strong-willed, and egotistical, but his accomplishments in forestry administration and his voluminous publications far outshone his unattractive traits of character.

On March 4, 1877, Carl Schurz entered Rutherford B. Hayes' Cabinet as secretary of interior. Schurz was born near Cologne, Germany, and was educated in the University of Bonn. In 1852 he migrated to the United States, where he had a mixed career as politician, pamphleteer, diplomat, and soldier before entering the cabinet. When he came to office the rather extensive and revealing forest survey for 1875 was already at hand and in dealing with public land and forest issues he could call on more data and support than any of his predecessors.

Secretary Schurz was a confirmed crusader for political and humanitarian causes, and in his position in the Hayes cabinet he demonstrated zeal for the challenge of managing the nation's resources. He initiated a reexamination of national land policies, to reveal the reckless waste of resources and to awaken a lethargic public to the importance of effective management at the federal level.

While Hough, Schurz, and Fernow functioned in the national capital, Charles T. Mohr, a native of Esslington, Württemberg, was active in the piney woods of the South. Mohr had arrived in this country in 1848 along with that wave of German immigrants who fled their homeland to escape political oppression. He had drifted into the South in 1857 and settled in Mobile, where he nurtured his botanical interests. In the heavily wooded gulf coastal rim he became enamored of the great southern pinelands. By 1880 Mohr had established his reputation as a botanist, a reputation materially enhanced in later years by the publication of a 900-page combination memoir and botanical treatise under the title *Plant Life in Alabama* (1901). In 1884 he had published part of his substantial pine report under the title *The Timber Pines of the Southern United States*, and in 1897 a much more complete survey, which appeared in the Department of Agriculture's revised *Bulletin 13*. Mohr's work, along with Filibert Roth's notes on the structure of woods, was to become a foundation document in the historical literature pertaining to southern forestry.

By 1890 Charles T. Mohr had become the best informed authority in the country on the South's timber resources. His survey of the gulf coastal Maritime Pine Belt presents a nearly definitive contemporary view of the virgin pinewoods before they were laid low by the big sawmills. In his introduction to Mohr's publication, B.E. Fernow wrote:

> The pines are the most important timber trees in the world. They attain their importance from a combination of properties. In the first place, they possess such qualities of strength and elasticity, combined with comparatively light weight and ease of working, as to fit them especially for use in construction which requires the largest amount of wood; next they occur as forest in the temperate zones, often to the exclusion of every other species, so that their exploitation is made easy and profitable; thirdly, they are readily reproduced and tolerably quick growers; and, lastly, they occupy the poorest soils, producing valuable crops from the dry lands, and hence are of the greatest value from the standpoint of the national economy.

These comments were to be substantiated repeatedly in the history of timber growing in the South, even down into its third forest era.

During the formative decades of scientific concern for American forest resources and conservation, the South, aside from the important contributions of Charles T. Mohr, had its own renaissance in other and somewhat surprising areas. In the late 1880s George Washington Vanderbilt, grandson of Cornelius, revealed decidedly more interest in animal husbandry, general farming, landscaping, and forestry than in high finance. He acquired more than 100,000 acres of rugged mountainous lands about the headwaters of the French Broad River in the western North Carolina counties of Buncombe, Henderson, Translyvania, and Haywood. This land was in the heart of the eastern slope of the Alleghany-Appalachian ranges, even though all of it lay west of the eastern continental divide. It was of rugged terrain, varying from deep moist coves and valleys to sterile balds at higher elevations.

Nowhere in North America was there a wider variety of deciduous trees, intermixed with a half-dozen varieties of conifers. Where the virgin stand of timber was undisturbed there remained in 1890 giant chestnut, yellow poplar, linden or basswood, black walnut, ash, maple, and nearly all the southern oak varieties. In these forested areas the autumn mast fall was heavy. Old timers still recall the fall seasons when chestnuts were gathered by the barrelfull.

There dwelt in the North Carolina highlands a race of eastern American mountaineers who for almost a century had existed in a state of social isolation. To George Vanderbilt and his numerous foresters and woodsmen these natives often presented more aggravating problems than did the management of the natural forest itself. From the outset Biltmore was confronted with three of the South's most persistent enemies—timber thieves, wild fires, and free-ranging scrub cattle and long-snouted woods hogs. It was an open question which of the three did the most damage to growing trees.

Even free of harm from men and animals, so vast a tract as the Biltmore Forest required diligent and expert management just to establish boundaries, spot overmature and deteriorating timber, open roads, and keep a lookout for squatters. No American forester had ever undertaken to survey, plat, and manage intensively so large a southern private forest landhold. Certainly George W. Vanderbilt was personally incapable of doing so. In 1892 his interest was centered upon the building of his famous French Renaissance castle on the French Broad River and the landscaping of the central part of his vast woodland domain. He sought professional assistance in the management of the larger and wilder mountain tracts, and consulted the famous New York landscapist Frederick Law Olmsted. Both Olmsted and B.E. Fernow recommended Gifford Pinchot as the most likely candidate. Pinchot was then already attracting some national attention, and before he went to Biltmore in 1892 had been employed in managing the Pennsylvania lands of Phelps, Dodge, and Company. Three years earlier he had returned from Europe, where he studied forestry in the French Forest School at Nancy and in the Sihlwald in Zurich.

Ostensibly George W. Vanderbilt's immediate interest was in having an exhibit prepared from the Biltmore Forest to be displayed at the Columbian Exposition in Chicago. This was to be Pinchot's first assignment. But when the young forester arrived in North Carolina in February 1892 he found the challenge much greater than that of a mere public relations project. Vanderbilt had organized his vast holdings from numerous small subsistence farms and wild mountain lands. They presented about every challenge that could confront a young forester. Many of the smaller valley tracts were still in cleared fields, which had to be reforested. Range animals took heavy toll of seedling stock, and annually woods fires damaged both seedling and mature trees. Even so, there remained many areas untouched by man and beast where virgin trees of large size and good quality stood. Again the task of surveying and establishing property boundaries was challenge enough to keep woods crews busy for several years.

Almost at the outset Gifford Pinchot learned a practical lesson that has been a part of the experience of every mountain timberland owner: there was a wide chasm between what was scientifically desirable and what in reality was achievable on the broken terrain. Logging the highlands of Appalachia has ever involved compromises between ideal forestry practice and the practical challenge of moving logs over treacherous hillsides to sawmills and then getting the lumber to market. Too, the European-trained forester at Biltmore quickly perceived that if left alone in a benign environment the eastern mountain lands, even on the hottest cliffside shoulders, possessed almost miraculous powers of recovery. Adjusting to the practicalities of the times in western North Carolina, Pinchot practiced logging operations of his own devising, combined with native-style conventional cutting of overage trees, with some success.

By 1898 Gifford Pinchot was chosen to head the Forestry Division in the Department of Agriculture, and persuaded Vanderbilt to employ a full-time, scientifically trained forester to replace him. That year Carl Alwin Schenck, a German forstmeister who had recently arrived in the United States, was employed to take over management of the Biltmore stand. Very soon after his arrival at the Biltmore Estate on the French Broad he discovered that the task confronting him was almost one of developing a forestry program from the ground up. In later years he wrote, "Vanderbilt had not seen any forestry—none in France, none in Switzerland, none in Germany, none in Sweden. He may have read about it occasionally, in *Garden and Forest*. I do not know." At the outset Schenck asked Vanderbilt for funds to finance the making of a topographical map of the 100,000-acre holding, which Vanderbilt refused. Despite his theoretical training Schenck was a man of practical views. His maxim was "that kind of forestry is best which pays best."

In the Vanderbilt forest Schenck had an excellent laboratory in which to demonstrate his philosophy. The huge privately owned tract could be opened to liberal experimentation without bureaucratic red tape and confusion. Though cautious about some expenditures, George Vanderbilt was responsive to intelligent planning and a program of continuing management. Not only did the Biltmore forest challenge a practical forester to demonstrate his capabilities, but at an early stage it became a readily accessible demonstration forest in which to operate an apprentice training program. In his autobiography Schenck said that the Biltmore Forestry School was conceived as early as 1896. It opened on a small scale in 1898, but it was not until 1902 that his dream was fully realized. A year earlier he had advertised the school, proposing apprenticeship experience in the Pisgah-Pink Beds area of the Blue Ridge and a three-month visit to European forests. In time about 350 young men worked in the pioneering training program. Many of these became practicing foresters, spreading the influence of the school through the south.

In imitation of the private German forestry training schools, Schenck undertook to produce scientific foresters who would be able to add a distinctly new dimension to the management of American forests. As forstmeister he was in complete control of the curriculum and training program. Students studied several of the master's textbooks and treatises, worked a year in the Vanderbilt woods, and then traveled abroad to view at first hand the work of European foresters. Fortunately a full file of letters from William E. Jackson of Lawrenceburg, Kentucky, describing the European visit of 1910 has survived. Schenck worked his students hard in the German forests and in the lectures. Bill Jackson found his trip abroad to be anything but a summer of leisurely enjoyment.

The Biltmore School, located southwest of Asheville in the Blue Ridge between Wagon Road Gap and Looking Glass Falls at Sunburst, succeeded for more than a decade, but suddenly in 1913 it was closed. In fact its existence had been threatened earlier because of a financial setback suffered by George Vanderbilt. Various reasons were cited for the school's closure, one being competition from publicly supported colleges and universities, another supposed friction between Schenck and the head of the landscape department at Biltmore. There was a lack of financial support, but the main reason, no doubt, was Schenck's periodic returns to Germany to fulfill his service obligations to the army. He remained head of the Biltmore Forestry School, however, until 1913. Schenck never became an American citizen, and throughout his years at Biltmore he was troubled about losing status with the German forestry authority and losing caste with his fellow army officers.

In its flourishing years the Biltmore Forestry School had an important impact upon the South and the nation. First, it helped to establish the concept that properly trained practitioners formed a profession, and that American natural resources responded to management and conservation. It spread its influence far and wide through its students and associates, who came to play an active role in the future of American forest management. The school's importance in the economic growth of the South and the region's social history can be summarized generally in terms of promulgating selective cutting and accurate cruising of timber stands, revelation of the annual disaster caused by forest fires and of the heartening capabilities of the southern deciduous woods to restore themselves after the removal of cattle and hogs, and demonstration of aggressive marketing procedures. As the Biltmore forester, Schenck made another important contribution to the western North Carolina mountains in the large importation of white pine seedlings from Halstenbek, Germany. The greatest contribution of the Biltmore School, however, was the southern forestry leaders it trained.

Joseph Austin Holmes, North Carolina state geologist, dreamed of the creation by the Federal Government of a large public forest in the Appalachian fastness in the western end of the state. Later his ambition was realized when in 1915 Mrs. George Vanderbilt sold most of the Biltmore mountain holdings to the federal government at a nominal price. This resulted in the creation of the Pisgah National Forest under the terms of the 1911 Weeks Law, which will be described in a later chapter. Holmes also crusaded successfully for the establishment of the office of fire warden for North Carolina in that year.

Forestry historians have tended to concentrate attention on the dramatic activities on the Biltmore lands along the headwaters of the French Broad and Pigeon rivers, and have neglected the rest of Appalachia. During the closing decade of the nineteenth and the first two of this century, speculators and timber exploiters were feverishly acquiring vast holdings in western Virginia, eastern Kentucky, and West Virginia. Among these buyers was the Interstate Investment Company, represented by the shrewd mineralogical engineer Rogers Clark Ballard Thruston of Louisville. Thruston spent the years 1887-1909 cruising the eastern face of Black Mountain in Kentucky and that area of the Cumberlands above Big Stone Gap, Virginia. In time he assembled a tremendously significant collection of plats and deed abstracts, which are as much social documents as evidence of legal land transactions. There were at least a score of other speculators, among them Warren Delano, uncle of Franklin D. Roosevelt, and the greatest land scout of all, John C.C. Mayo of Paintsville, Kentucky, who bought hundreds of thousands of acres of prime timber and mineral lands. Perhaps no other individual in Appalachia, with the possible exception of George Vanderbilt, bought and sold such vast tracts of fine virgin hardwood timber. Down the pine Mountain range about Middlesboro and Pineville, Kentucky, English and Scottish promoters bought and managed vast tracts, and hoped some day to establish on their holdings an idyllic English recreational and industrial community. Speculative activities of the same kinds were occurring in East Tennessee.

With the exceptions of the Interstate Investment Company and the British speculators, none of these buyers seem to have made a modern timber cruise of their property. In 1907 Thruston had a professional appraisal made of the timber stand on Interstate's holdings on Black Mountain in Kentucky and above Big Stone Gap in western Virginia. This analysis, no doubt the first one ever made in Kentucky, was produced by A.B. Patterson of Chittenden and Patterson, consulting and contracting foresters of Baltimore. The report on these lands constitutes a remarkable description of Appalachian woods that had scarcely been touched by mountaineer owners. The forester listed over 36 million board feet of prime timber ready for harvesting, and a wide variety of trees.

It was in this era that the great log runs were taking place on the mountain rivers, and the sawmills were advancing upstream to meet the rafts. Unhappily this area was without pioneering foresters, such as those at Biltmore, to introduce sound management and conservation principles. As the timber was harvested by the most primitive mode of selection and logging, fully half of it was wasted by ignorant loggers. There never emerged in this part of the Appalachian highlands a conservation crusader comparable to W.W. Ashe and his colleagues in western North Carolina, even though the two areas were only a few mountain folds apart.

North Carolina was fortunate to have within its borders a man like W.W. Ashe, one of the South's ablest scientists and most public-spirited sons. He was a native of Raleigh and a graduate of the University of North Carolina and Cornell University, 1891-1892. Upon his return to the South he became a pioneer naturalist. From 1892 to 1913 he was associated first with Gifford Pinchot and then Carl A. Schenck at Biltmore. He participated with them in the first experiments conducted in the fields of silviculture and forest management. Later, as a practicing forester, he encouraged Charles H. Herty, a University of North Carolina chemist, to make an analysis of that state's turpentine pines and the resin extracting procedures. Ashe suggested that a better method of gathering gum should be sought, a suggestion that led to the invention and perfection of the Herty cup or box.

In a close examination of the Pisgah Forest timber stand, Ashe added to the list of known species and subspecies of trees and shrubs by at least a hundred new entries. He also introduced to both the country and the South a concept of the importance of selective cutting of mature trees and more conservative logging procedures. He, like Pinchot, was cost-conscious in the harvesting of timber. Perhaps Ashe's most enduring personal contribution was his dogged campaign to help secure the enactment of the famous Weeks Law in 1911.

Ashe and his contemporary colleagues were stirred by the monotonous fire losses. Flagrantly evident down into the third decade of this century were the contributions of southern illiteracy, superstition, folklore, and shameful public indifference to losses of forest and soil resources. No one can ever know what it cost the region annually in timber and erosion losses to tolerate broomsage field burnings to flush out hillside rabbits. Farmers set fire to their fields to free them of scrub pines, insects, and snakes; by these practices they also undertook to hasten the greening of spring grasses in lean hillside pastures, to save herds of skeletal cattle that survived the winters. All these things Holmes, Ashe, and their colleagues knew and crusaded against. There was no worse region in the country for constantly setting the woods on fire than southern Appalachia. In his analysis of the timber stand on Big Black Mountain in Harlan County, Kentucky, A.B. Patterson, the Baltimore forester, gave a graphic description of the fury of an uncontrolled fire. He wrote: "In the fall of '96 a fire came over Big Black Mountain from the North, burned over the slopes as far west as Nims Hollow Branch, skirted around the heads of Raesor and Clover Forks, burning over a great deal of Big Black Mountain and Middle Ridge and crossed over Little Black Mountain a short distance East of Potato Hill."

By the opening of this century more and more people had become fully aware that if uncontrolled wild fires, current wasteful modes of timber harvest, and deep soil erosion were not stopped both the nation and the South would run short of lumber and forest products within half a century. But in this age of laissez faire political and economic philosophy the challenges were too great to be undertaken on a national scale. The conservationists of the era focused on two abused areas, the White Mountains of New England and the southern Appalachians.

The first quarter of the twentieth century was, from the standpoint of both destruction and reclamation of much of the South's forest resources, one of the most important in regional history. At the end of this period many of the big mills had cut out, and even the small "peckerwood" operations were winding down. Southerners could now view on their native soil evidence of the harsh fate that had earlier befallen the New England and Great Lakes woods.

The statistical tables in 1920 still indicated that the South appeared to have a considerable surviving timber resource, and its potential for growth seemed high. Statistics of this kind, however, were at best deceptive indicators of the true situation in the woods. They did not make historical comparisons with the large volume and high quality of 1880, nor did they indicate the impact of the phenomenal removal of prime quality trees on the fate of the land. Further, the tables gave no hint of the extended interval of time necessary for a second forest to sprout and mature to a condition comparable with the first. Although no dependable quantitative statistics seem to be available, it perhaps would not be a gross overstatement to assume that by 1924 less than 10 percent of the original volume of conifers and deciduous trees listed in 1880 was still in the woods. That part of the southern economy which was based upon the timber harvest suffered severe reduction after 1921. By then the saga of the big sawmills was rapidly fading into history.

An important event that stirred earlier regional awareness of forest management was the meeting of the Southern Forestry Congress in Asheville, North Carolina, in 1916. The organizational meeting of this body was encouraged by the Society of American Foresters and the American Forestry Association. At this date the South lagged far behind the other timber growing regions of the nation in the enactment of conservation legislation and the promotion of forestry education. Southern public reaction in this field had scarcely been stimulated, and in the statehouses old-line agrarian-minded legislators remained uninformed and indifferent. At that date only five southern states either had organized forestry commissions or had done anything publicly in the areas of management, regulation, and research.

At the initial meeting of the Southern Forestry Congress Joseph H. Hyde of North Carolina was elected president, and the organization embarked upon a crusade of encouraging the southern states to catch up in the areas of forest management. In 1916 the South was beset by the existence in its Maritime Pine Belt of hundreds of thousands of acres of cutover lands. So far no one had come forward with a practical plan to relieve the loss of income from too-heavy lumbering practices. Equally pressing concerns were loss of industrial payrolls and accompanying unemployment, the reduction of state and local revenue, and the continuing fire losses.

A prime example of a major lumber-producing state in trouble was Mississippi. In a summary history, Jack Holman, a Mississippi State forester, wrote, "Steam-powered skidders with long cables dragged the logs from the stump to the rail siding. This process tore at, broke off, and often dug up young trees in the path of these logs. This type of operation left the land bare with stumps as the only reminder of what was once there . . . beautiful stands of trees. The bare soil began to erode and small rivulets grew into gullies."

The Mississippi Federation of Women's Clubs had already organized a crusade to promote fire control, to conserve the remaining stand of virgin timber, and to preserve the land. They also began a movement to reclaim the blackened lands by initiating a planting program for the development of their state's second forest.

Compared with the giant operations of the huge sawmill entities the efforts of the Women's Clubs, though modest, were remarkably effective. At the outset of the women's campaign Mississippi was losing annually to forest fires more capital worth than it expended on all of its institutions of higher learning. Fortunately the adoption of the Nineteenth Amendment to the United States Constitution in August 1920 gave the Mississippi women a powerful political leverage. They supported the beloved Henry L. ("Granny") Whitfield, president of the Mississippi College for Women, for governor and won. In 1926 the Mississippi General Assembly enacted legislation creating the state's Forestry Commission, and for the first time Mississippi began to take serious notice of the conservation of its great forest resources.

In the original forestry law the Mississippi Legislature appropriated $12,000 to the support of the new commission; the Federal Government, under terms of the Clarke-McNary Law, contributed $8,000, and, it was said, the American Forestry Association supplied an equal amount. Legislators instructed the new agency "to take such action as is necessarry to prevent, control and extinguish forest fires, including the enforcement of any and all laws pertaining to the protection of forests." The new division was also entrusted with the responsibility of carrying out two more objectives of the Women's Club crusade: to encourage the planting of trees and to stimulate public interest in forest management.

Across the South the Mississippi experience was repeated in one form or another. It took considerable effort to get redneck legislators, long steeped in shoddy factional politics, to grasp the importance of reforestation or to see that such a thing was possible. They were reluctant to enact enforceable fire and grazing laws for fear of offending equally ignorant voters. After 1920, however, conservation-minded citizens began to arouse broad public concern. Today, a southern legislator would court defeat if he arose from his seat and asked, as did a brash South Carolina "statesman" in 1922, "What is forestry?" By the beginning of the Great Depression ten southern states had created forestry commissions, and were prepared to take advantage of the assistance offered by New Deal legislation in the fields of reclamation and conservation.

A little over a decade after the Southern Forestry Congress was organized it joined with the American Forestry Association and state foresters to organize, in 1928, a group called the Dixie Crusaders.

This organization set out to inform country people in Georgia, Florida, and Mississippi of the importance of their forest resources and of the damages caused by fires. In order to get their messages across the Crusaders produced two documentary movie films, *Pardners* and *Danny Boom*, and they equipped motor vans to transport lecturers and equipment to even the most isolated communities.

In 1930 a Dixie Crusader van visited the piney woods community of Junction, Florida, a place too small to be recognized by the United States Post Office. There was no building adequate to contain the crowd, and the meeting was held outdoors. "Many of the people who came," said the lecturer W.L. Moore, had "never before seen a motion picture—several had never heard of such a thing—so there was considerable interest and excitement." The pictures were projected onto the side of the local store, and the storekeeper, who acted as chairman, observed, "There ain't been this many people in Junction since the day George Miller got shot."

The picture and Moore's lecture provoked a vigorous comment from an old Florida cracker who might well have spoken for people in all three states covered by the Crusade. "Folks," he said, "I been living here in these woods all my days and I can recollect when we had no fires. Our cattle were fat then, and we drove them to Tampa to market. We drove so many that the grass was leanin' that way all the time. And we had money—somethin' we ain't got now and somethin' we ain't never goin' to have long as the woods is burned up. Just last week some scamp put out fire on my place and burned my shed down. I tell you, folks, we ain't got a thing, none of us, and if we want our kids to have anything we got to stop this burnin'!"

During the two years of the Dixie Crusaders' campaign they distributed over a million and a half posters, book covers, and handbills, lectured to almost two million parents and school children, and presented 632 picture shows. Half a million people viewed the exhibits and the lecturers and projectionists drove thousands of miles in their vans to reach people who had never heard a warning word against woods fires. This whirlwind campaign must be considered a highly successful venture.

Immediately after 1920 there developed across the South a distinct lull, if not depression, in the region's economy. Farmers suffered serious reverses as results of falling cotton and tobacco prices, boll weevil damage, loss of markets, and a faltering credit system. Rapidly the wasteful post–Civil War staple-crop economy fell upon even leaner times. The long history of crop liens, furnishing store financing, and share tenancy came to a close almost simultaneously with the end of the big sawmills and wanton exploitation of the virgin pine forest.

Bankruptcy for the South in 1925 was a grim spectre, especially for little farmers and sharecroppers. Long before the onset of the Great Depression nationally most southerners had met their economic armageddon, as was documented eloquently by legal notices of forced sales of land to satisfy mortgages and tax delinquencies. Public notice columns of country newspapers and courthouse bulletin boards blossomed with notes of blighted hopes and the economic despair of the old agrarian system. Exhausted farm lands and cutover timber tracts could be acquired at buyers' bargaining prices. The land was only worth what a prospective purchaser said it was worth to him, not what it had on it. Some wornout and deeply eroded cotton plantations of five hundred to a thousand acres sold for as little as a thousand dollars, and in some cases perhaps half that amount.

Thus the South in 1920 was ripe for a sweeping economic reappraisal of its immediate past history, a revolution in the management of its forest resources, and the development of new land use policies. Measured in terms of long-run future growth this might be considered one of the most fortunate reversals in southern history. Absence of a flourishing lumber market slowed down the final harvesting of the still existing first forest, and failure of the old agricultural system focused attention upon the wasted land. Standing by silently to aid in the erasure of the scars of human folly were the tenacious loblolly and shortleaf pines. Within a decade and a half they had covered many an acre of washed out and exhausted and abandoned land with a saving mat of straw, had begun to check erosion, to flatten old cotton rows, and even to obliterate the sites of ancient farm homes and tenant-farmer cabins. Far more significant was the departure from the land of people who had known no other way of life for generations than cotton farming and its impoverishing economic mores. While pines sprang up in many parts of the pine belt South, the Appalachian highlands were also on a road to partial recovery by vigorous new growth of deciduous trees.

The southern forest industry in the mid-1920s was stuck on dead center, powerless to function at more than a token volume, and it was not yet prepared to approach the future with certainty that a profitable second forest could be created. The reports of the United

States Census for 1920 and 1930 did not include a single cord of southern yellow pine pulpwood converted into a cellulose product other than elementary kraft paper; there was only a limited manufacture of plywood, and no compressed composition or pebbleboard.

Yet, as early as 1884, the tiny South Carolina Fibre Company had announced it was able to reduce pinewood to soft fiber by using the sulphate process. Behind this pioneer beginning of diversified wood usage was the rich human story of Major James Lide Coker, once a student of Louis Agassiz in Harvard University. He served as an officer in the Confederate Army until he fell wounded in the battle of Lookout Mountain and was captured. When he was paroled the disabled Coker's mother hauled him home to South Carolina in a farm wagon. He recovered and over the years became one of the New South's most imaginative entrepreneurs. In 1884, with his son James Lide Coker, Jr., he organized a company to attempt utilization of the common pinewood so readily available about Hartsville. The Cokers early began the manufacture from kraft paper of cones on which local textile manufacturers wound their yarns, but this was the start of a long and frustrating process of experimentation.

The Cokers faced two major problems in their efforts to establish a successful paper mill at Hartsville in the 1890s. First was that of building a cooker whose lining would withstand the "eating" effects of strong sulphuric acid. The one they bought of the New York American Sulphite Pulp Company had a defective lining, and it was not until James L. Coker, Jr. did considerable experimenting with a ceramic and sand lining that the Hartsville Company was able to overcome this weakness. The second problem was the resin content of the local pinewoods. In 1892 James L. Coker, Jr. purchased of Pusey and Jones, New York City, the first papermaking machine to be built in the South for the precise purpose of chemically processing pinewood pulp. When the machine was installed in 1893 it worked fine—except that the wire screen accumulated a hard coating of resin that was difficult to remove either mechanically or by use of chemicals. In time this problem was overcome sufficiently, by experimenting with various pinewoods and discovering the best cutting season, to permit the manufacture of coarse kraft paper for wrapping and industrial uses.

There seems to be little historical justification for not declaring the Cokers the southern pioneers in the making of kraft papers from pine stock. There is a historical marker in Roanoke Rapids, North

Carolina, however, which declares that the "First Kraft Pulp in the United States was made here by the sulphate process using southern pine in 1909 by the Roanoke Rapids Manufacturing Company." The author of this inscription perhaps allowed local pride to override historical fact; or perhaps there is some unspecified difference between the Coker process of manufacturing kraft paper and that used later by the Roanoke Rapids Manufacturing Company.

In subsequent years local paper mills were able to produce enough sulfate paper to enable a weekly newspaper to print a special edition proclaiming the future economic glories of the South when at last its pinewoods would be used to sustain a southern press. This early pine paper, however, was of an unattractive greasy brown appearance with a sticky texture and unpleasant odor. Even a boasting editor before 1930 surely knew that the time of production of a satisfactory newsprint from southern pine pulp was still in the future. More chemical research was required before plentiful pine fibers could be transformed into attractive and sophisticated printing stock and other forms of commercial papers.

Caught up in the economic depressions of the early 1920s and the Great Depression of the 1930s, the South had one ray of economic hope. The era of its second forest was dawning. This was a period of revolutionary changes when there was a general awakening on the part of thoughtful southerners to the challenges of the new age, challenges that demanded a redressing of past follies with an advancement of the new sciences and technologies to insure future social and economic well-being.

5. Inception of the South's Second Forest

Lumber operations in the great southern coastal pine belt at the turn of the century were controlled largely by hard-fisted and myopic men who, if they ever thought in terms other than producing the greatest amount of lumber in the shortest possible time, kept their thoughts to themselves. They focused strictly on hauling logs from the woods and delivering lumber to purchasers wherever on the globe they could be found. There was no time in this competitive and frenetic drive to plan for the future, which they would not be around to greet anyway.

One in this throng of lumbermen, however, stood out as an exception. He was Henry Hardtner of Urania, Louisiana. Gauged by standards of the leviathan mill operators of the South, Hardtner was a modest timberman and mill operator. Nevertheless his impact on long-range southern forest management, restoration, and policy-making was of impressive magnitude. Next to Charles T. Mohr he was possibly the most farsighted person in the longleaf pine belt in those years.

Hardtner, like Mohr, was of German extraction, the son of an immigrant shoemaker and country merchant who had settled immediately after the Civil War near Pineville, Louisiana. Pursuing a more or less natural economic course for the place and time, the Hardtners early engaged in sawmilling, first as buyers of stumpage, then as timberland owners. Certainly young Henry Hardtner was not the first southerner to realize either the disastrous rate of depletion of the virgin timber stand or the possiblity of renewing the resource. He was, however, a pioneer in the area of the Gulf Coastal Old Southwest. In 1905, aside from Charles Mohr's publications, virtually no scientific information was available about the capability of the longleaf pine to replenish itself from natural seeding and to thrive under proper care on cutover lands.

Three decades later, speaking before the Society of American Foresters in New Orleans in December 1931, Hardtner said, "At first I had to pioneer every step in my investigation of the reproduction of longleaf pine. I thought it would take 60 to 100 years to grow a merchantable crop. No one could tell me what was possible, no yield tables such as you have now were then available. I had to work out the problem for myself."

In his self-directed approach to forest renewal Hardtner tried at least three experiments that proved successful. He established a sane dimensional scale-at-breast-height to guide his loggers, and he stuck to the rule. He ordered that three or four healthy mother trees be left standing on each acre logged. He then attempted to use more careful logging procedures. Hardtner, along with other Gulf Coast lumbermen, was aware of the severe damage caused by at-large hogs and by the perennial firings of the land. He perhaps knew that longleaf pines produced viable seed crops only every four to eight years. In addition Hardtner determined that much of the Louisiana cutover lands were not really adaptable for agricultural purposes. When he told the Society of Foresters that he had learned about timber growth from close observtion of the life cycle of the woods themselves he was describing a method that still has genuine validity, even in the face of tremendously advanced knowledge of silviculture.

In the context of the early years of this century, and in comparison to most southern lumbermen, Henry Hardtner no doubt appeared to be a foolish and impractical dreamer. The "practical" sawmill operator of the period neither knew nor took time to learn anything about the science of forestry. Not only was Hardtner a pioneer in the management of his Urania stand, he carried his ideas and crusade to the state capitol in Baton Rouge. Louisiana's General Assembly, at his nudging, enacted a law in 1904 that authorized organization of a department of forestry, though this proved an empty gesture. Four years later Hardtner was appointed to a commission for the conservation of natural resources by Governor J.Y. Sanders. This opened to Hardtner a new public channel for exchange of ideas in forestry conferences, and the means of getting over to Louisiana farmers and timbermen some knowledge about their surrounding woods. Later Hardtner was made chairman of the commission. His major influence, however, was in blazing his own private course to the future through the Urania experiments. Surprisingly, W.W. Ashe, on a visit to Louisiana in 1909, could impart to Hardtner little of the advice and information he sought. Ashe appeared skeptical about the experiments he saw on the Urania lands, but he respected the zeal and ability of his host.

Hardtner stuck by his lonely crusade. In New Orleans in 1909 he addressed the Conservation Conference for the Southern States with fervor. He exhibited knowledge of regional forestry conditions. He estimated the forest area in the thirteen southern states to be 208.8 million acres. This enormous acreage, he said, should be managed in such a manner that young trees would quickly replace the large annual cut of virgin stock. He contended that the South already had all the forest stand it needed; the existing forest had only to be properly protected. Prophetically Hardtner told the conservationists: "The future of the South is bound up in the forest preservation with its accompanying protection to watersheds, power streams, and woodworking industries; not only in the protection of the watersheds, which will some day furnish the power of the great majority of the manufacturing establishments but in the prosperous continuance of industries depending upon forest products." He anticipated both the philosophy and arguments put forth in Congress two years later in the Weeks Law debates.

Other conservationists addressed southern assemblages with equal enthusiasm. Two of these were Frederick J. Grace, register of the Land Office and Commission of Forestry for Louisiana, and R.S. Kellogg, assistant forester in the United States Forest Service. These men advocated conservation of existing timber resources and the restocking of cutover lands by seeding. Like Hardtner, they found it difficult to make a satisfactory impression upon audiences attuned to past practices.

Historically one of Henry Hardtner's most effective accomplishments was promotion of the Louisiana forest renewal tax. As a senator in the Louisiana General Assembly he was able to bring about the enactment in 1912 of a tax-deferral law by which land devoted to reforestation would be assessed at a fixed annual rate for twenty years, with the privilege of a ten-year extension if timber stands had not matured sufficiently to be harvested. As the timber was cut the owner was to be assessed an established severance tax rate. Hardtner was the first to register his cutover lands under this contract tax arrangement. This was an area where he had a more tangible influence than in speaking to public audiences.

In 1917 Hartner invited Herman H. Chapman and his Yale University forestry students to spend their spring term in Urania. This was the beginning of an association that was to last for several years and to prove a constructive experience for both Urania and Yale. He also led to the establishment after 1921 of a sub-branch of the Southern Forest Experiment Station. Henry Hardtner also served the cause of southern forestry as chairman of the Southern Forest Research Advisory Council for a decade, and he was a leader of the Southern Forestry Congress from its inception in 1916, serving as chairman of the forestry committee of the succeeding Southern Pine Association.

In an informal appraisal of Hardtner's work at Urania Philip C. Wakeley, the salty Southern Forest Experiment Station–Great Southern Lumber Company forester, spoke of him as a shrewd businessman who had a grasp of the future. By 1924 Hardtner's Urania mill was sawing second-growth fixed-assessment timber. Wakeley regarded the Urania mill as a ramshackle establishment. "He had," said the forester, "an old rattle trap mill and Urania, the town, was nothing to look at. In fact, you'd have to look carefully to find it today. But the mixed lob-lolly, shortleaf, dash-of-hardwoods type with islands of longleaf in it around Urania was the center of the Yale camp for years, and having started his program he utilized to the full the advice of Chapman and other members of the Yale faculty." Wakeley concluded, "So there was a nucleus, a focus of happy affection, so to speak, at Urania, dating back roughly to 1912, and that undoubtedly had something to do [later] with Sullivan and Goodyear's [Great Southern Lumber Company officials] starting to look into things in Bogalusa." Henry Hardtner's enthusiasm and persistence in the field of advanced forest management caused many people to take a second look at their timber stands and the reclamation of their cutover lands.

The Urania experiment was not only famous for its pioneering effort at conservation in an area where it was of such vital importance, but also paralleled a major public crusade to conserve forest and land resources. While Hardtner and his associates campaigned to invoke general support for conservation of timber resources on the part of individuals and companies, much larger effort was being made at the national level. An area considered by the conservationists to be best suited for the acquisition of an eastern national forest reserve was the southern Appalachian hardwood belt. They proposed the acquisition of vast areas of land already occupied by homes and farms to form protective headlands above navigable streams, this land to be permanently administered by the federal government. For the South, as for much of the Far West, this proposal was a reversal of land policies. Only within recent past decades virginal areas of timbered public lands had gone begging for purchasers.

Hardtner published his views on the acquisition of a national hardwood forestry reserve at the time when the subject of the Weeks Law or Appalachian Bill was being publicized in the conservationist journals and debated in Congress. The movement favoring this law began well back into the era of growing concern for the preservation of the nation's timber resource, and the rise of scientific forest management. In his statement on "How the National Forests Were Won," published in *American Forests* (October 1913) Gifford Pinchot made the observation that to date the United States had not developed even the semblance of a forestry code such as the one used in France, or those of the other advanced western European countries. Instead Congress plastered laws on top of laws with too little regard for either their administration or unfortunate implications. For example, there was the benchmark amendment of 1891, tacked on to the general land bill, which gave the president power to reserve forested tracts within the public domain. This amendment was voted into law, paradoxically, at a time when the Congress had been for more than three decades recklessly and fraudulently ceding enormous tracts of public lands to special interest groups. Already invaluable tracts of first forest lands had slipped beyond public control.

The timberland frauds, said Pinchot, had by 1891 become gargantuan. To correct a part of this error a national forest committee, with Charles Sprague Sargent as chairman, was appointed. This group visited the Far West and selected 21 million acres of timberlands to prevent a total loss to the public of a vital natural resource. This committee no doubt opened the way for setting two important precedents, that of revising some land distribution policies, and of either reserving or purchasing large blocks of land from Indian reservations to be held in a national park reserve. These included the Platt National Park, 1902, the National Bison Range, 1908, and the Montana Bison Range, 1909, all of which gave material support to the debates concerning the constitutionality of the proposed Weeks Law.

During the first decade of this century the battle to purchase and reserve large blocks of forest lands in the mountainous regions of the United States was joined by the American Forestry Association and an impressive number of organized conservationists on one side, against timber and railroad men, mineral speculators, and conservative politicians on the other. In the meantime the national forest reserve under the Reserve Act of 1891 and the subsequent Forest Management Act of 1897, which was called by some The Magna Carta of American Forestry, had reached a peak of approximately 190 million acres. It was against this briefly outlined backdrop of broader national legislation that the Weeks Bill for the reservation of two relatively large mountainous areas in the East was formulated. In the formative years 1881-1910, Americans and at least three of their presidents came to view the nature of their continent and its resources in fresh perspective.

Nature organizations, from bird watchers to forest conservation bodies, were formed in ever-growing numbers. In addition, commercial clubs and local trade associations were formed to represent mixed and private concerns with recreation, tourism, related service businesses, and conservation. Among these was the Appalachian Mountain Club. This group was organized before 1900 and was a leading supporter of the first Appalachian Bill, which was introduced in the Congress in 1899 by Senator George Pritchard of North Carolina. This bill proposed the creation of a southern Appalachian restricted forest area out of "absolute forest" lands in the southern highlands. W.W. Ashe estimated that approximately a seventh of the areas of Virginia, Kentucky, Tennessee, North Carolina, and Alabama were in this category. To the north, a comparable situation prevailed in Maine and New Hampshire.

At the moment when the discussion of the Appalachian Bill was becoming intense John H. Finney, secretary of the Appalachian Forest Association, wrote in 1909, "Today, no southern state has an acre in state forest. . . . Surely all the states must finally resolve to have forest acres under competent foresters; must enact adequate fire laws; must properly tax forest lands, and must do other things as are necessary to the perpetuation of the South's large and enormously valuable area now in the hands and under the control of individual owners bent on cutting them."

The discussion of the Appalachian Bill took place in the sunset moments of the Speaker Cannon domination. Joseph Gurney Cannon, a native-born North Carolinian, and his old-guard clique in the

Congress made passage of any progressive legislation difficult, and the Appalachian or Weeks Bill faced rugged opposition from the outset. Questions were raised as early as 1909 as to whether the federal government could legally acquire forest lands under the constitutional provision for improving rivers and harbors. This no doubt was a sincere question. In the course of the debate in 1911 on this vitally important bill and the inclusion of the White Mountains, however, a small-bore Ohio congressman, Paul Howland, made the accusation: "Thus it appears that New England has clasped hands with the southern Appalachian states, all past sins have been forgiven and forgotten, and in the sacred name of conservation, we are witnessing one of the best organized raids on the Federal Treasury in history."

Notwithstanding Congressman Howland's malevolent waving of the sectional "bloody shirt" in what may have been its farewell appearance, the Appalachian Bill stumbled its troubled course through both congressional and public debates.

President William Howard Taft personally supported drives to halt the destruction of the mountain forest. He wrote Albert Shaw, editor of the *Review of Reviews*, on April 30, 1909: "Our children and their children will not be able to make headway if we leave them an impoverished country. Our land, our waters, our forests, and our minerals are the source from which come directly or indirectly the livelihood of all of us. The conservation of our natural resources is a question of fundamental importance to the United States now, to the business of man today." Geographically Taft was in a position to know about conditions in Appalachia because Cincinnati was one of the centers of speculation in lands in that area.

The final draft, which Congressman John W. Weeks of the Tenth Massachussetts Congressional District introduced in 1910, was essentially a composite of compromises. Primarily its intent was the protection of navigable Appalachian streams from erosion and silting of their watersheds.

In the long period of discussion of this conservation issue down to 1910 the focus was purely upon the watersheds and timber stand in the southern highlands, but when the bill was drafted in its final form it included the White Mountains, where the pine forests had been cut over and logged almost to the point of depletion.

During the congressional session of 1911 there ensued a heated debate over every aspect and implication of the Weeks Bill. Proponents of the bill introduced the testimony of the experts: George F.

Swain, civil engineer, Harvard University; L.C. Glenn, geologist, Vanderbilt University; and Filibert Roth, School of Forestry, University of Michigan, and a contributor to Mohr's *Bulletin 13*. Their collective and impressive testimony was convincing and perhaps a decisive factor in the enactment of the law. The bill had the support of much of the newspaper and periodical press, foresters, and state officials. Proponents argued that with the inclusion of the White Mountains the impending Weeks Bill was given a national scope of application. "The bill," said the editor of *American Forestry*," involves an issue of national equity and appeals strongly to the national sense of equity without regard to the section or party affiliation."

The law as enacted in the evening of March 1, 1911, was no doubt less comprehensive than had been the original intent. T.W. Sims and Finis Garrett of Tennessee passionately opposed the bill. On the other hand Asbury Francis Lever of South Carolina delivered an effective concluding summary to the debates in support of the law. In the final vote only three Tennesseeans—Cordell Hull, John Byron Austin Moon, and L.P. Padgett—and two North Carolinians—John M. Morehead Grant and E.W. Pou—voted in favor of enactment, and no Kentuckian was listed as favoring it. In what appears to have been a strange and short-sighted action the Congress appropriated $1 million for 1910 (a year already passed) and $2 million for each of the next four years, the grant to be terminated in 1915. These special funds were to be used to finance a cruising of properties, determining boundary surveys, and the acquisition of Appalachian and White Mountain lands located about the headwaters of navigable streams.

To carry out the intent of the Weeks Law, a seven-member body bearing the title National Forest Reservation Commission was appointed. It was to be composed of the secretaries of interior, agriculture, and war, along with two members of the House and Senate. This commission was authorized to approve all land purchases. The secretary of agriculture, through the department's Bureau of Forestry, was given responsibility for actually locating the lands, devising purchase agreements, and certifying the validity of titles. The law admonished the secretary to refrain from purchasing productive farm properties and to strictly observe certain regulations.

A concern as to the constitutionality of creating national forests still lingered in the minds of congressmen. The argument was that Congress could dispose of public lands, but lacked authority to purchase them back from private owners. Proponents of the law scotched this argument by saying, "The nation that can purchase lands for national parks, as has been done several times, can purchase lands for national forests to maintain a permanent timber supply, protect our waterpowers and preserve the national health, whether such forests affect the navigability of navigable rivers or not." It was decided by the Supreme Court in the Gettysburg case (purchase of the battlefield) that the national government could purchase land for "the inculcation of patriotism."

Almost immediately upon the presidential signing of the Weeks Law the United States Forest Service busied itself with the location and purchase of mountain woodlands. At the outset the question arose whether the $1 million appropriated for 1910 was still available? On top of this confusion the $2 million appropriated for 1911 had to be spent in less than nine months. By June that year foresters had located one and a quarter million acres that were available in the two mountain areas covered by the law; actually only 31,377 acres were cleared for immediate purchase.

Federal land agents quickly came to appreciate the fundamental facts about landownership in the southern Appalachians. In thousands of cases people could establish little more legal claim than squatter occupation to the unsurveyed and unregistered tracts on which they lived. Boundaries were imprecisely marked and described as extending from one impermanent set of landmarks to another, most of which had long ago vanished. Many boundaries in fact had never been established; many titles and descriptions were ineptly drawn by half-literate hill-country lawyers and county surveyors.

Traditionally it was a practice among many Appalachian landholders to establish in their deeds fewer acres than they actually claimed, in order to reduce tax bills. This led, and still does, to endless labors and litigation in the purchase of mountain lands. Added to the legal complexities that arose from sly folk dodges was the overwhelming physical task of locating boundaries and corners on rough and almost inaccessible terrain. Foresters who purchased lands during the first year of application of the Weeks Law paid from $1.16 to $15.00 an acre, or an average of $5.95, which in 1912 was a tempting price to most ignorant and land-poor mountaineers. The quality of the lands and forest cover often varied dramatically. Some were largely denuded of saleable trees, while others were still covered with mature commercial trees. This was especially true of the highland regions of western Virginia, West Virginia, eastern Kentucky and Tennessee, western North Carolina, and northern Georgia. Much of the timber in West Virginia and Appalachian Kentucky about the bituminous coal fields was rapidly depleted to supply mine timbers.

If the establishment of property boundaries and verification of title vexed the federal foresters, the meticulousness of government lawyers in Washington aggravated them more. The Forest Service quickly discovered that news and rumors spread far and fast in Appalachia, and purchases of Appalachian lands had to be consummated before third parties intervened and drove up prices. It was impossible to hasten the examination and certification of large numbers of individual titles through the cumbersome federal system. So the Forest Service largely abandoned the practice of negotiating purchases and establishing title in the traditional manner, and resorted to massive condemnation proceedings to secure court-ordered commissioner deeds. This in no way disrupted negotiations with the landowners as to the price ultimately paid for the land, or forced them into a sale. It was simply a legal method of dealing with an otherwise impossible situation of establishing land titles.

In time the Weeks Law underwent substantial amendment. The first revision was made in March, 1913, when the administration of easements and right-of-way and other administrative problems threatened the management of headwaters property in areas of access and improvement. These matters were placed directly under the administrtive control of the secretary of agriculture. The terms of the law were liberalized to permit the purchase of properties along streams and well below the headstream watersheds. In 1922 an exchange law was enacted, which broadened the federal government's acquisition capabilities. This new law permitted the exchange of government-held timberlands especially for those held in cutover areas in the southern pine belt. Thus the Weeks Law along with the exchange law was said to have placed the United States Forest Service in a more favorable position to acquire desirable and contiguous lands. Henry Cantwell Wallace, secretary of agriculture, wrote in the following year:

> The Forest Service, in administering the provisions of the general exchange act, has primarily in view building up the timber growing resources of the national forests. Increased facility of administration and better protection from fire and other sources of damage are often valuable benefits but do not receive primary consideration. Under no circumstances

are exchanges approved for the benefit or convenience of owners of private land, and a clear-cut benefit to public interest is required before any exchange is given serious consideration. The attitude of the Forest Service in approaching and handling this exchange work has been one of great caution and conservation.

Few commentaries on the public need for timber conservation and the encouragement of intelligent reforestation and management contained more practical observation than did that by the director of the Forest Service in the senior Wallace's administration. Both the secretary and director cautioned legislators and the American people that the republic was coming uncomfortably close to destroying its vital wood supply. Wallace warned that the per capita rate of wood consumption in 1920 required four acres, producing fifty cubic feet of wood annually, "This production of wood," he said, "cannot even be approximated unless we become skilled in the art of growing and managing forest products with economy."

By the early 1920s there were both public and private pressures to expand the government public forest holdings. In 1924 a more enlightened and bolder Congress enacted the Clarke-McNary Law. Now freed of the ominous threat of unconstitutionality which had so seriously hampered the framing and passage of the Weeks Law, the drafters of the Clarke-McNary legislation could address the broader issue of acquiring and managing public forest lands with a bolder philosophical thrust.

Basically the new law was an outline or blueprint for securing the cooperation of the states with the federal government in areas of fire control and prevention, the protection of greatly extended watersheds and stream courses, the devisement of modern timberlands tax laws, and prior examination by the United States Geological Survey of lands being considered for purchase. The way was opened for individuals to make private gifts of lands to the federal preserves, and the president was further empowered to enlarge national holdings, and especially those used by the armed services. Responsibility for examining reports of prospective purchases and all other matters pertaining to the public forest administration was placed in the hands of the Secretary of Agiculture, who in turn was to be the chief reporting official to the National Forest Reservation Commission, especially in matters pertaining to the location and availability of lands. The heart of the Clarke-McNary Law was emphasis upon cooperation with the states.

Between 1911 and 1933 the national Forest Service was able to establish acceptable titles to more than 3.2 million acres of mountain, submarginal, and cutover lands in the South. The National Forest Reservation Commission approved purchases in the region in these decades of 5.8 million acres. These purchases represented a tremendous bargain for the federal government. Over the entire period the average price paid per acre was $3.89, a significant reduction from the $5.95-acre average paid in 1912. Reflected in the lower average price were soil exhaustion, farm failures during the Great Depression, and the out-migration of hundreds of thousands of southern tenant and submarginal farmers.

By 1979 the total of federally owned forest lands in eleven southern states had increased to 24.5 million acres, and almost twice this area was outlined for future purchase and addition to the national forest holdings. This goal may be unattainable in the face of currently inflated land prices, increased competition from corporate purchasers, and the awareness by private owners of the importance of conservation and management. Much of the four-dollar land of 1933 now sells from $300 upward per acre.

The purchase of the rather large forest tracts under terms of the Weeks Law placed an ever-growing burden upon Forest Service personnel to locate, survey, and haggle over prices with landowners, and to establish validity of titles. The Clarke-McNary Law fundamentally liberalized several aspects of national forest management, and certainly enlisted the support of the states to conserve forest resources. The ultimate plan of public forest enlargement appears on every southern state map in the large colored areas surrounding the actual national forest lands owned and administered by the federal government. These shaded areas, however, must now be considered no more than an expansive dream.

Imprinted in bold letters on the state maps mentioned above are the regionally intriguing names Nantahala, Unaka, Pisgah, Choctawhatchee, Sumter, Francis Marion, Daniel Boone, Ouachita, Ozark, Great Smoky, Homochitto, and many others. These public forests signify a reversal of national land policies from those promulgated by the Congress in the opening of Indian lands on the frontier of the Old Southwest in the early nineteenth century. The purchase of public lands signaled a happier future.

History came full circle in the South. In the application of the provisions of the Weeks Law an appreciable potential forest renewal area was restored to permanent public control rather than being left to waste away in sterile gullies, denuded mountain slopes, or beneath the cover of worthless brush and trees. During seven decades of Weeks Law history much of the national forest area in the South has undergone a phenomenal reversion from badly abused cutover lands to moderately well managed preserves of growing timber, a fact that contributes materially to the social and economic welfare of both the region and the nation.

In the Roosevelt-Taft era naturalists bubbled over with enthusiasm for restoring the American forests, and they had a significant impact on the shaping of resources policies. By 1910 the first forest in most sections held out only dim promises of continuing to be a mainstay for wood supply, and the future was up to the conservationists and scientists. An increasing concern on the part of some federal agencies, some congressmen and senators, and some private landowners was for the development of more scientific information about conservation, timber restoration, and management.

On the land and in the woods almost any laborer could readily identify varieties of trees, differentiate roughly between commercially sound logs and worthless culls, guess fairly accurately standing board measures, and conduct crude logging procedures. More expert timber cruisers, however, could estimate well within the standards in use at the time the annual per-acre increment. They did this almost altogether in terms of surface guesses at profitable and unprofitable cuttings. Few foresters or lumbermen in the South in 1911, however, possessed scientific knowledge of the seeding rhythms, life cycles, and growth of both pine and hardwoods, or the making of large-scale woods analyses. The few companies that concerned themselves with conservation and forest renewal were without dependable data derived from carefully directed research and experimentation.

Two concerns dominated the drive for southern forest restoration. First was the discovery of some method of recovery at reasonable cost of the vast coastal and piedmont crescents of cutover and abandoned pinelands, and the reestablishment of the deciduous growth in the Appalachian highlands. Second was the general conservation of southern soils and the stabilization of regional economics. In July, 1921, Congress and the Department of Agriculture set out to meet these challenges.

In that year the Southern Forest Experiment Station was established by the federal government with its main base of operations in New Orleans. The legislative creation of this new forest agency was the result of considerable pressure from several interested groups in the South, but especially from the lumbermen's associations. The agency's first budget was a meager $17,900, which had to be stretched thinly over efforts to achieve the broad objective, "to study the growth and yield of the southern pine." The agency hired four trained foresters and a clerk to accomplish this mission across the coastal and piedmont regions from South Carolina to Oklahoma and Texas. The first director of the station was R.D. Forbes, who was thoroughly conversant with the extent of devastation wrought by the great mills. In his first year as director he prepared a dramatically descriptive essay, which was published in the March 1923 issue of *American Forestry*. He conveyed on paper a graphic sense of the ghostly desolation that characterized thousands of square miles of a once-noble virgin forest. Forbes' article was all the more poignant because he cast it in terms of human and regional disaster.

Almost immediately following 1921 three substations were established: one at Asheville, North Carolina, one at McNeill, Mississippi, near Bogalusa on the Pearl, and a third at Starke, Florida. Later other field stations were placed at Bogalusa, Urania, and Crossett, Arkansas. In carrying out the general mandate of Congress and the Department of Agriculture, the Southern Forest Experiment Station was entrusted specifically with the tasks of studying fire damage and devising means of prevention, growth analyses, and determining the general effects of grazing animals upon forest restitution. In the latter case the infant agency was thrown immediately into conflict with southern backwoodsmen, who from the time their scraggly forebears had brought their hogs and scrub cattle to the piney woods frontier had regarded the mast and roots of the open woods as a God-given legacy to themselves and their animals.

Aside from these perennially nagging questions there was the larger one of finding how best to fill in the cutover void. For two decades or more this had been a primary topic of discussion by lumbermen and conservationists who met in conventions to discuss the future of the timber industry. Always the twin menaces of fire and at-large livestock were highly visible, but not so the importance of artificial reforestation, woods management, the making of timber analyses, and the gaining of a scientific understanding of the life cycles of southern forest trees. These were matters that demanded the talents of both practical and theoretical foresters. Almost as vexing a problem as the cutover lands for the staff was how to accomplish anything within the spartan budget. During its first decade the Southern Station's staff was increased to twenty-four members to serve the main and substation operations, and had under way an analysis of southern conifer and hardwood resources. In 1931 test cruises were made on 500,000 acres in eastern Louisiana and southwestern Mississippi. By that time the station had begun the publication of research bulletins and articles giving the results of staff findings.

Little was known about the actual reproductive capabilities of the forests, beyond the fact that old-field pines would in time reclaim abandoned cotton fields. Even the gathering and care of seeds, the planting and care of nurseries, and the transplanting of seedlings were virtually fresh topics for research. Nature was a wholly unpredictable ally; it took years of patient research to determine so elementary a fact as the most productive spacing of planted trees. A historical landmark of this era of experimentation was the preparation and publication of Philip C. Wakeley's *Artificial Reforestation in the Southern Pine Region* (1935). Two decades later he published his enlarged report on the subject under the title, *Planting the Southern Pines* (1954).

Scientists of the Southern Forest Experiment Station concerned themselves not only with basic matters of silviculture but with soil conservation and flood control. The station's list of publications grew annually. Examples are J.D. Sinclair, "Studies of Soil Erosion in Mississippi," a paper read before the Society of American Foresters in 1930, Russell R. Reynolds, *The Crossett Story, the Beginning of Forestry in Southern Arkansas and Northern Louisiana* (1980), and Philip Wakeley, "Geographic Source of Loblolly Pine Seed," *Journal of Forestry* (1944).

The creation of the Southern Forest Experiment Station was an important reversal of past practices. Its scientists have examined subjects ranging from soils and geography to plant genetics and profitability of various tree types. In many ways its activities have paralleled fairly closely those of the agricultural experiment stations and the work of the extension services in the areas of crop and livestock production. Aside from the actual research findings in the fields of silviculture, soil conservation, and suppression of enemies of the forests, the agency has served the cause of southern forestry in another important area. Over the years there has been a constant coming and going of staff members in all branches of the service. These for the most part have been employed by state and corporate forestry agencies, which have gained materially from this reservoir of trained people.

During the sixty years of its existence the Southern Forest Experiment Station has performed the necessary laboratory and field research to permit publication of specialized bulletins, papers, research notes and field maps, and the indispensable annual *Pulpwood Production in the South*. Few agricultural field crops, with the possible exception of cotton, have received more intensive attention since 1921. The bulk of the Southern Station's literature has appeared within the past two decades. These eloquently document the fact that the South is challenged to produce a maximum amount of wood fiber from a constantly shrinking land area devoted to forest culture. By 1984 it seemed there were few if any more secrets locked inside the bark of southern pine trees.

While the Southern Experiment Station has influenced the social and economic history of the South, it has by no means accomplished this work alone. Four or five important lumber industry groups made significant contributions. The first of these, aside from Henry Hardtner's work, was the Great Southern Lumber Company (1909) at Bogalusa, Louisiana. This big industry straddled the heartland of the gulf coastal pine belts of Louisiana and Mississippi.

Great Southern officials, like all other coastal lumbermen, faced the ultimate exhaustion of their virgin stand of pine, and then of either reforesting cutover lands or following the current trek to the great woods of the far Northwest. Foresters undertook to have enough mother trees left per acre to insure reseeding. The company's logging procedures, however, precluded this practice; steam skidders knocked down and butt-scarred every young tree in sight. Too, viable seed crops could be expected in the longleaf belt only every four to eight years, and then it was doubtful that enough kernels would penetrate deep enough into mineral earth to sprout. Always on hand to destroy the natural seedlings were the ubiquitous twins of decimation, hogs and wild fire.

Great Southern foresters experimented with natural seeding, hand seeding, and the planting of nursery-grown stock. By 1923 the company had planted a million seedlings on 3,700 acres of land, and in addition its foresters and workmen patrolled 103,580 acres in efforts to control destructive enemies. Even so the company suffered severe damage to 7,317 or more acres of young trees that had been nursed through the initial stage.

During the summer of 1922 Dean J.W. Toumey of the Yale School of Forestry examined the Great Southern stand of remaining virgin timber along with the reforested areas. He suggested, first, that the remaining virgin stand had reached full maturity and should be harvested. In his opinion no further profit could be derived from holding such timber for future use. He even suggested that the company exchange much of its virgin timber for established second-growth stands.

Toumey reasoned that a growing second-growth stand on such a large area, staggered over a quarter of a century, would produce a continuing supply of wood. He said future harvesting operations should be planned so as to take advantage of favorable seasons and seed production. Uttering a long threadbare warning he admonished the company to control hogs and firings. Aside from these, two of the greatest menaces were fire-spreading steam skidders and logging locomotives. Toumey told Great Southern's officials that in those areas of their stand where enemies of the trees had been controlled since 1921 there was a healthy restocking.

Natural seeding in the Great Southern's cutover lands was the most inexpensive approach to reforestation. This practice, however, could not always be adopted; instead there had to be considerable assistance by artificial planting. This necessitated the operation of a nursery and dependence upon cultivated rather than natural stock, and even an adaptation of different species of pines.

In summary the Yale professor told the company's officials: "The large area of absolute forest owned by your company with some twenty-five years cut of virgin timber ahead, offers one of the greatest, if not the greatest opportunity of continuous operation to be found among private holdings anywhere in the country, if the attitude of the officers of the company toward sustained yield, and their apparent willingness to make present expenditures for attainment, make economic success reasonably certain provided provisions for regrowth are made at the proper time and the techniques or methods followed are such that will result in stocked stands at the lowest costs." If the Great Southern officials were patient enough to read through the professor's bumbling sentence they could be assured they had received sound advice.

By 1923 the term "regrowth" was rapidly becoming a key to sustaining continuous lumber operations in the South. Most, however, simply continued in the indifferent attitudes that led to their earlier devastations of the eastern and Great Lakes stands, and looked to the far northwest for new virgin forests to lay low. Russell R. Reynolds, veteran director of the Crossett (Arkansas) Experimental Forest Station wrote, "In any event, by the middle to late 1920s, the end of the big cut was near at hand, and by 1930 many of the mill owners who had come South after logging in the Great Lakes had been completed, started looking at the big untapped virgin stands of the West as the location for their next operations."

Reynolds arrived in New Orleans in July, 1930, a recent graduate of the University of Michigan School of Forestry. He was assigned to the Southern Experiment Station's economic division and in 1932 to the Crossett and Arkansas project. He first worked with the Ozark-Badger case study, and then in the Crossett Lumber Company stand. This was in the years of the Great Depression, and the southern lumber companies, like those at Bogalusa and Crossett, were faced with serious problems of timber renewal if they expected to continue operating in the South.

By 1933 the South's big lumber industry from Wilmington to Houston faced numerous problems, none of them more important than a revolution in logging operations. The days of the old-style steam procedures were numbered. The skidder had, historically, proved to be highly destructive, and the logging locomotive with its fire-belching stack was too expensive and destructive to remain an acceptable means of transportation. The Crossett Lumber Company and the Southern Forest Experiment Station formed a cooperative pact to work with a 25,000-acre block of timber in the making of a close analysis of the stand in terms of cutting, lumber yield at the mills, cost of harvest, and the ultimate dollar return from the operation.

These experiments involved an assessment of ultimate acre yield of profitable logs, selective cutting practices, and utilization of wastage of inferior logs. As part of the revolution then coming to the southern woods the motor truck was first employed to transport logs. The solid-tired vehicles were in use in other forms of transportation, but few or no lumbermen knew how successfully they could be operated on muddy and sandy log roads or over rugged terrain, or whether they could be depended upon to deliver a sufficient quantity of logs to supply a big mill. Of course, their cost of operation would be a major factor.

That year the Crossett Lumber Company offered the Southern Experiment Station three sections of second-growth pinelands to be operated as an experimental forest. In time there came from this substation an important volume of information on the profitability of second-growth stock, utilization of southern swamp hardwoods, diversification of wood uses, cutting cycles, hauling logs and lumber by motor truck, aerial fire patrol, genetic experiments, and controlled firings.to suppress underbrush. Although many of the experiments carried out at Crossett substation were being conducted simultaneously in other places, collectively its work was of broad importance to the entire southern wood-using industry. No other agency was more successful in developing a cooperative arrangement between private industry and public research programs.

A revolution in timber management in the South had occurred since Henry Hardtner began his crusade to restore to productivity the pine forests of Louisiana. The drive to secure passage of the Weeks Law, the beginning of the national forests, and the establishment of the Southern Forest Experiment Station and the Bogalusa and Crossett substations occurred concurrently with the rise of the modern paper and other non-lumber-using forest industries in the region. The migration of the timber industry was reversed and a second inmigration began. This time modern wood-using industries came to stay. They purchased vast acreages of timberland, built enormously expensive processing plants, employed highly sophisticated forest management techniques, and gave close heed to those golden terms of wood-using industrial survival, "regrowth" and "continuous operation."

6. The CCC Boys

At mid-decade of the 1920s the South had arrived at a major crossroads in its history. This was the point of no return to the days of reckless agricultural practices or the slashing away of the magnificient first forest. Gone were the days when furnishing merchants supplied the region's agrarian credit needs at ruinous rates of interest and prices for goods. If there was any hope left for little cotton farmers it was too dim to illumine the future; the simple truth was that both tenant farming and the old style sawmill and timberman had outlived their time. No longer was the sawmill industry capable of serving as a safety valve for a dangerously deteriorating social system and regional economy.

In some fashion every major social problem in the South had grown out of the land and its mismanagement. The land, which had spawned agrarian failure, and that part of it lined with the stumps of the virgin first forest now haunted the pillagers and robbed their heirs of a birthright. Never in the whole scope of southern history had such a large proportion of the land been caught in so harsh a crisis as that caused by defective farming practices and runaway erosion. Added to these problems was the recurring one of floods, which swept away annually untold millions of dollars of wealth.

One of the most destructive forces of the depression era was the disastrous reduction of the southern tax base. The impoverishment of the land resulted in the reduction of taxes collected and of institutional support. In Florida, Stuart A. Campbell, of the University of Florida College of Commerce, wrote in 1934 that out of slightly more than 35 million acres 5 million were considered worthless by owners and tax assessors; most of these had become a burden on the state. Although the abandonment of depleted farm and timberlands had not advanced so far in the other southern states, they also were approaching a crisis condition. When the Franklin D. Roosevelt Administration came to office in 1933 the rapidly growing rate of abandonment of gutted and sterile farms in the South presented one of the most vexing social and economic problems facing the New Deal emergency agencies.

At the national level in those famous "one hundred days" of the New Deal there was also a staggering burden of unemployment, and in the South, as elsewhere, the ranks of the unemployed included hundreds of thousands of youth between the ages of seventeen and twenty-five years. The record is not clear as to who suggested employing these youth in a natural resources conservation program; the idea may have come from Roosevelt himself. In those feverish early days of the New Deal the recommendation for the organization of an Emergency Conservation Work program was sent to Congress, which enacted the law authorizing it on March 31, 1933. Roosevelt's message recommending it strongly implied that something more fundamental than mere conservation work in the national parks and forests was involved. He emphasized that getting unemployed youth out into the woods and fields in units of approximately 250 men would have a great moral and spiritual impact.

The initial appropriation request for funds to support the youthful corps was for $300 million to be drawn from the unexpended balance of the 1932 fund for the relief of destitute persons, plus $10 million of new money. Five days later the president issued an executive order to begin immediately the organization of the new emergency agency.

Congressmen and senators could only have had vague notions what the Emergency Conservation Work Corps was supposed to do. Not even President Roosevelt at the outset was sure what the mission of the Corps was, except to put men to work immediately. He said in his message introducing the program, "The overwhelming majority of men who are walking the streets and receiving private or public relief, would infinitely prefer to work."

The law creating the Emergency Conservation Works Corps provided that it would participate "in the construction, maintenance and carrying out works of a public nature in connection with reforestation of lands belonging to the United States or the several states which are suitable for timber production, the prevention of forest fires, floods and soil erosion, plant pests and disease control, the construction, maintenance or repair of paths, trails, and fire lanes in the national

parks and national forests." The president was given wide discretionary powers to extend these services to states, counties, and even private landholders.

Four departments—War, Interior, Labor, and Agriculture—bore
almost equal responsibility for the organization, operation, and administration of the mini-army of youth. Fortunately the National Forest Commission played a leading role in planning the work. The soils
survey unit of the Department of Agriculture was most constructive
in outlining projects.

Recruits for the new emergency work force were enlisted very
much as if they were volunteering for military service, and the woods
camps were operated as quasi-military units. The important difference, however, was that recruits might drop out at any time, and for
those who remained the period of service was six months. Regimen
in the camps was somewhat more relaxed than was the case in the
army. Enrollees were given physical examinations, issued military type
fatigue clothing, and sent off to basic orientation stations located in
established army camps.

The first Emergency Conservation Works Corps contingent was
dispatched from Washington on April 17, 1933, to Luray, Virginia.
These first 2,000 youths lugged with them an elementary manual
hurriedly drafted by foresters who undertook in fifth-grade language
to explain the strange phenomena of the woods, the modes of using
various tools, and the descriptions of poisonous plants and snakes.
It was a challenge of the imagination to illustrate in a book the skills
of chopping, sawing, and felling a tree to boys who never in their
lives had witnessed such an operation. Too, there was the matter of
divesting youthful minds of nursery-book horror stories of the woods.

This first work corps was assigned to the George Washington National Forest along the Virginia-West Virginia border. When the men
arrived early in the morning amidst a downpour of rain to establish
Roosevelt or Camp No. 1, the prospects were just about as unprom-
ising as they could have been for city-bred youth. These same grounds
three quarters of a century earlier had presented equally grim prospects to other youths in the Civil War campaign. The greenhorn contingent from the nation's capital had to clear away the underbrush
and trees from the site to establish camp, the first of hundreds of such
installations across the continent. An agile lad climbed and topped a
swaying pine sapling and attached halyards for the hoisting of the
camp flag. A field kitchen was put in operation and a hot meal gave

a moment of relief and improved the perspective on what seemed from the outset a dubious undertaking. First Sergeant R.H. Nesbit, an old army hand, soon had staked off a company street, issued tools and plans, started the construction of a permanent kitchen and tool shed, and established something approaching military order and routine. No man was compelled under military rules to remain with the corps for the full term of his enlistment, and Sergeant Nesbitt said the first days quickly separated from the service those youths either too timid or too lazy to work.

Roosevelt's original proposal seemed to anticipate the enrollment of 250 to 300 thousand men. By September 1933, 365 thousand had enlisted, and most of these had remained in the service. By December that year 1,486 camps had been established. Discussions were under way in Washington as to how a projected 4-million-man force could be profitably employed in conservation work. (There were, however, never more than 360 thousand at any one time. Members of the Emergency Conservation Works force were paid from $30 to $40 a month, and about $22 of this amount was sent home to support dependent families. In addition the men were supplied shelter, food, clothing, transportation, medical care, and access to additional education.

The first annual report of the director of the corps contained a listing of over 500 classes of services rendered during the first six months of its existence. These ranged from making firebreaks, building fences, and opening trails to timber surveys and the stocking of lakes and streams with fish. The national map was generously dotted with campsites, and the service overspent the original $300-million allotment. The country was laid off in corps areas conforming with those established by the United States Army. The southern states were located in the third, fourth, fifth, seventh, and eighth districts. The Fourth Corps Area was made up entirely of eight southern states, and was assigned an original quota of 3,800 men, but 4,386 enrollees were enlisted. The forested areas of the South offered one of the most serious challenges to the Corps, but at the same time comprised an excellent field of operation in keeping with the stated purposes of the Act of March 31, 1933.

The national director of the Emergency Conservation Works agency was a vital man of varied experience. Robert Fechner, of third-generation German extraction by way of Pennsylvania, was born in Chattanooga in 1876 and was educated in the public schools of North Georgia. Briefly Fechner was enrolled in the Georgia Institute of Technology. His most important training, however, took place in Augusta as a machinist apprentice. For a time after completing his apprentice training Fechner was employed by the Central of Georgia Railroad, and from 1914 to 1925 he served as an official of the International Association of Mechanics. Fechner moved to the East Coast where he became an expert labor negotiator and dispute settler. He was active in political affairs in Boston and lectured in the Harvard School of Business and in Dartmouth and Simmons colleges. On April 5, 1933, Roosevelt appointed him director of the new conservation agency, a position he held until his death in 1939.

Fechner proved to be a most effective choice for this position. He had broad enough experience both in work procedures and with labor relations to maintain harmonious relations within the highly diversified army of youthful workers and with a mixture of administrators in Washington. At the same time he proved to be a hard-nosed director of few words but with great respect for almost endless statistical details. Ten days after Fechner took office the number of southern camps was increased from the original 33 to 198. By the end of the year this number was greatly expanded. In the Tennessee Valley alone 25 camps were placed about the headstreams of the central river system, and in time the number of southern installations ranged from 48 in Virginia to 18 in South Carolina.

Late in December 1933 Hugh H. Bennett and Edward C.M. Richards made a preliminary report on the watershed area of the projected Norris Dam in the Clinch basin. They said parts of "The Tennessee River basin are fast becoming the 'bad lands' of the East." Their early survey covered nearly two million acres, which formed the valleys of the Powell, Clinch, and Cove Creek. Nearly half of this area had been farmed, but by 1933, said Richards, had been "absolutely destroyed by farming." This meant that a monumental task of erosion control and reforestation awaited the 20 Emergency Works Conservation Corps units assigned to that area.

In the South, the main work of the Corps was concentrated in the areas of halting erosion on abandoned farmlands, bringing devastating forest fires under control, opening roads and trails, and planting trees.

A federal program that benefitted directly from the work of the Corps was the Tennessee Valley Authority, which was created on May

18, 1933. That summer 25 conservation units were assigned to the upper valley for the making of general preliminary surveys of needs and to institute a wide assortment of conservation practices. Around the headstreams, where once existed a magnificient forest of hardwoods, much of the land was now denuded of forest cover, as Bennett and Richards had reported. Bennett, in an article in *American Forests*, October 1934, wrote, "Every year the area thrown out of cultivation is increased despite the fact that many fields are annually recleared of the second-growth pine, persimmon and sassafras that sprang up following the previous cultivation and abandonment." Annual flooding and resulting erosion were uncontrolled.

In the decade from 1933 to 1943, the corps did almost all of the basic work in these areas mandated in the legislation creating the Tennessee Valley Authority. In this instance the conservation corps was granted authorization to work directly with both private and public landholders. One of the necessary procedures was the procurement of permission from stubborn southern private landowners to open fire roads and trails across their property.

Late in 1933, New Deal legislation also created the Soil Erosion Service Division in the Department of Interior, under the direction of Hugh H. Bennett. This service published a horrendous map of the effects of erosion in the United States. Almost the entire South appeared on the face of the map under the bleeding categories of "serious" and "harmful widespread erosion." In the famous soils specialist's traditional forthright manner he stated: "It is recognized by erosion specialists familiar with the geographical details of the problem that much of the abandoned eroded land of the nation has passed beyond the possibility of practical reclamation for crop production. On these lost areas not much effort will be spent at present." This was a harsh condemnation of the old way of agriculture and life in the South. For several decades prior to the coming of the New Deal, county extension agents across the South had preached almost to deaf ears a doctrine of terracing and land conservation. The tradition-bound region clung to the eighteenth-century assumption that an unlimited supply of virgin land would be available, and the average illiterate southern farmer and his tenants regarded the mysteries of the spirit level as beyond ordinary human comprehension. The building and maintenance of terraces is a difficult task, requiring constant attention, and the average southern farmer was not accustomed to applying so much energy to the maintenance of his land. Finally, large areas of Appalachian and sandy piedmont ridges of the South were so steeply sloped that no amount of terracing would alone check erosion and runoff. In almost all of these areas land values were so depressed as to discourage farmers from expending funds and energies in conserving them. In extensive portions of the older cotton belt, where the ratio of sharecroppers to owners was high, there was an unbelievable indifference to the future of the land.

Hugh Bennett wrote early in his new assignment: "We have made very general surveys only in these regions and consequently have only rough estimates of the damage. Recently I found on practically every slope cultivated long enough for the stumps to have decayed that either clay subsoil or gullies are in evidence all the way from the vicinity of Birmingham, Alabama, to Bristol, Tennessee. In one section twelve miles long, it was estimated that eighty-five percent of all cultivated lands as far east and west had been ruined." In this instance Bennett was writing specifically about the area of the Tennessee Valley, but he was equally familiar with the soil conditions of the cotton and tobacco lands, where often the ravages of erosion were more evident. Supplementary to Bennett's surveys the later Farm Security Administration reports reflected a region rapidly rushing headlong into a state of soil bankruptcy. R.S. Maddox, a former Tennessee State Forester, said that in some of his state's counties 80 to 90 percent of the cultivated lands had been ruined by erosion. W.W. Ashe, the famous North Carolina forester, estimated that the Tennessee stream system washed away annually 11 million tons of soil to be deposited on downriver sandbars and in the Gulf of Mexico.

This was the situation in most of the depression-burdened South in April 1933 when the Emergency Conservation Work force set out across the region in its great experiment of conserving both human and natural resources. In the seven state Tennessee Valley region the work force labored to control erosion, to reconvert denuded Appalachian slopes to forest and grass-covered lands, and to check heavy rainwater runoff.

Though there were large areas of public lands in the upper valley, most of the erosion control and forestry renewal work had to be performed on private lands. This proved to be the case throughout the South, a fact that required considerable revision of the Emergency Conservation Act of 1933. On June 28, 1937, Congress enacted a revised law that gave the president greater leeway in carrying out the purpose of the conservation agency.

The revised law of 1937, which created the title "Civilian Conservation Corps," was liberalized almost to the extent of authorizing publicly employed personnel to work on private lands under the discretionary powers "of doing thereon such kinds of co-operative work as may be provided by the acts of Congress, including the prevention and control of forest fires, forest trees pests and diseases, soil erosion, and floods." It was provided that any project undertaken on private property should be backed by assurances that the improvements would be maintained in the future.

It was evident from the outset that none of the ravages of forest and land resources were respectful of private versus public land boundaries. The CCC was granted wide latitude to institute all reasonable and necessary procedures to combat fires, pests, and erosion, irrespective of whose land was involved. There was urgent need for the construction of lookout fire towers on the most strategic sites. Roads and trails were constructed on contiguous rights-of-way, and other types of access ways were opened across properties of varied ownership. By 1940, eighteen CCC forestry camps were still in operation in the great Valley, where men were employed in checking erosion and in expanding the historic tree nurseries at Clinton, Tennessee, and Muscle Shoals, Alabama.

In undertaking to control runoff waters that slashed hillside gullies and deposited burdens of silt on lowlands, the CCC constructed hundreds of miles of fascine check dams. These were staggered down slopes and across gullies in such a manner as to check the flow of rainwater, to trap silt, and to permit grasses to take root. The CCC discovered that in one instance, at least, an East Tennessee farmer had deliberately created deep gullies on his property by plowing furrows up and down hill in lieu of building fences around his pastures. In some extreme cases corpsmen, using Abney terracing levels, found that cornpatch farmers were undertaking to cultivate slopes inclined by as much as eighty percent. By the end of its eighth year the CCC had not only completed dramatic erosion control projects, it had planted 62 million trees on 40,000 eroded acres located on 8,500 separate Tennessee River watershed farms. Following these highly visible demonstrations private farmers were induced to plant 11 million additional trees. The CCC had also fought 114 major forest fires.

It is difficult to isolate in Fechner's annual reports specific details that related to the South alone. The first southern labor quota, established in April 1933, was 64,825 men who were distributed among 47

Above, rafts up the Troublesome–North Fork of the Kentucky River; *below*, bunching logs by mule power in Appalachia, about 1910. *Alice Lloyd College*

Above, poplar logs bunched behind a splash dam under a denuded ridge; *below*, splash dam on Ball Creek, Knott County, Kentucky, about 1915. *Alice Lloyd College*

Above, ox and mule logging in a virgin whiteoak forest; *below*, log rafts on the Kentucky River, about 1912.   *Dunn Collection, Kentucky Historical Society*

Opposite, logs and a sawmill on the Kentucky River at Irvine. *Dunn Collection, Kentucky Historical Society*

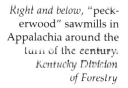

Right and below, "peckerwood" sawmills in Appalachia around the turn of the century. *Kentucky Division of Forestry*

Above, longleaf pine forest in LaSalle Parish, Louisiana, about 1900. *American Forests*

A Georgia turpentine worker cutting a box. *U.S. Forest Service*

Right, the Herty box in operation. *U.S. Forest Service*

Above, a boiler afloat in the Big Sandy River, on its way to a sawmill deep in Appalachia. *Alice Lloyd College.* *Below*, mine timbers at the entrance to a shaft in Kentucky. *Kentucky Division of Forestry.*

Above, a planing mill with its burning tower destroying shavings, 1950s. *Kentucky Division of Forestry.* *Right*, lumberyard at Ford, Kentucky, 1914. *Wilson Collection, University of Kentucky Library.*

Above, pulp chips being loaded from chipper to railway cars at a modern sawmill.   *Kentucky Division of Forestry.*   *Below*, lumber camp near Hazard, Kentucky, about 1918.   *Dunn Collection, Kentucky Historical Society.*

Above, four wooden ships under construction at Tampa, 1918; *below*, launching of the *Nacogdoches*, named by Mrs. Woodrow Wilson, at Houston, 1918.   *Manufacturers Record*

Students at the Biltmore Forest School, 1910.
Courtesy of Susan Jackson Keig

The Civilian Conservation Corps at Camp Roosevelt, 1933.   *American Forests*

A gully in South Carolina, 1935.   *U.S.D.A. Soil Conservation Service*

A gully in wornout cotton land, planted by the CCC with black locust seedlings, 1937.   *U.S.D.A. Soil Conservation Service*

Above, building the tool house at Camp Roosevelt, 1933. *American Forests.* *Right*, a CCC fire-tower, now a fire-control museum piece. *Richard G. Stone, Jr.*

Above, a southern hillside reforested by CCC boys.   *American Forests.*
Below, corpsmen planting trees on deeply eroded lands in Tennessee.
Tennessee Valley Authority.

Above, a "third forest" stand of young hardwoods, crisscrossed by skid trails; *right*, bulldozer skidding pine logs over rough terrain. *Kentucky Division of Forestry*

Above, pine logs being loaded in the old-fashioned way, 1958; *below*, loading prime hardwood logs with a mechanical skidder.   *Kentucky Division of Forestry*

White pine plantation on exhausted farmland. *Kentucky Division of Forestry*

A young loblolly pine plantation.
Richard G. Stone, Jr.

Mother trees amidst clear-cut
pinelands.

Above, planting improved loblolly pine seedlings on a prepared site; *below*, pine seedling nursery beds in South Carolina.   *South Carolina Forestry Commission*

Above, the pulpwood truck has replaced the cotton wagon in many parts of the South. *Below*, a mechanical loader lifting pulpwood from a woods truck.

Loading pine pulpwood in an assembly yard.

Transferring pulpwood to a truck for the trip from woodyard to paper mill.

Left, pulpwood cut from young stock.   *Below*, mound of pulpwood behind a paper mill, 1960.   *Kentucky Division of Forestry*

Above, Bowater Southern newsprint plant on the Hiwassee River at Calhoun, Tennessee. *Tennessee Valley Authority. Below*, a papermaking machine at Weyerhaeuser's Columbus, Mississippi, complex; this machine is capable of producing a 24-foot ribbon of paper 900 miles long every 24 hours. *Weyerhaeuser Company.*

Above, Land Between the Lakes, looking across the Barkley Dam pool of the Cumberland River; *below*, strip-mined land in the Tennessee Valley, nine years after reclamation.   *Tennessee Valley Authority*

work camps. Nationally there were 259 camps with 201,806 men. In 1940-1941 there were 424 southern camps out of 1,508 nationally, which accommodated 342,101 men in the South. The statistics of enrollment reflected the facts that the South was among the most active regions in the country in the enlistment of youth, and their record of serving out full terms of enlistment was good.

Though Fechner's staff annually prepared elaborate statistical tables that described the multiplicity of CCC activities, the various services performed in each of the nine corps areas were not clearly distinguished. The bulk of the work in the southern states was concentrated on soil conservation, reforestation, and making a biological survey. Since large areas of the coastal and internal swamps of the South were vital habitats for wildlife, the CCC undertook to restore refuges and to make these areas more inviting and secure for feeding and nesting shore birds and animals. Robert Fechner wrote in 1938, in next to his last report, that "the starting of the CCC almost simultaneously with the beginning of the national effort to save the wildlife resources was indeed fortunate."

During the first five years of the existence of the works corps it planted more than a billion trees on approximately a million acres of devastated cutover lands. Foresters in 1938 estimated that there remained 26 million acres of land nationally that should be reforested— a task, it was said, that would occupy a comparable corps for many years in the future if the work were properly performed. In this year southern CCC enlistments were at their peak, often exceeding original allotments to the region.

Up to this point discussion of the impact of the CCC on southern lands and forests has been couched largely in statistical terms. The more important and lasting accomplishments, however, must be evaluated in terms of the intangible results of breaking isolation barriers, changed attitudes toward the land, introduction of a sense of modern conservation, and the impact upon southern family life at a moment when needs were greatest. No one, not even Robert Fechner with his statistical tables, could truly assess the impact of the CCC on the general human welfare and economic recovery of the South in the late 1930s.

This branch of the federal emergency relief program could not have come into existence at a more propitious moment. So far as basic conservation programs were concerned, most of the states had developing departments of forestry and were mounting substantial campaigns to accomplish one of the central objectives of the federal forest conservation act, the control of wild fires. Larger segments of the southern population were being drawn into the informational crusades and were being enlightened about the rapid depletion of the last vestiges of the region's great virginal resources. At the current rate of harvest in the late 1920s it was estimated this would take place within the next generation.

In his final report, written late in 1939, Robert Fechner said that since 1933 the CCC had planted across the United States more than 1.5 billion tree seedlings. It had gathered 582,089 bushels of pine cones and nuts, and 11.7 billion pounds of acorns. He wrote in the manner of a man who sensed that he was delivering his valedictory. He looked back over the six and a quarter years he had directed the Corps and summed up its accomplishments in terms of almost miraculous results. This was even more dramatic when it is remembered that the manpower of the organization was for the most part young, raw, and untrained for work in the woods and on the land. Every six months the CCC started all over again with a fresh crop of green recruits, who had to be instructed on how to perform even the simplest tasks and how to use tools designed for more sophisticated laborers.

In addition to the general administrative challenges of handling so large an organization of green workmen under relatively lax military discipline, private landowners and country people in general had to be convinced of the long-range importance of the Corps to the future of their communities and region.

In 1937 rampant nature brought down upon southerners of the Ohio and Mississippi Valleys a harsh demonstration of the importance of erosion control, soil conservation, and reforestation. The devastating flood of that year necessitated the occupation of 23,300 CCC corpsmen in emergency rescue and revetment work. They were engaged in sustaining levees, in rescue missions, and scores of other emergency activities. They transported supplies, sustained medical aid, and remained behind when the waters subsided to help reestablish families in new homes. During the three-week peak of emergency involvement, the CCC supplied 2,000 trucks and spent more than $4 million on various phases of relief work. There could have been no more impressive or timely revelation of the dire necessity for erosion control and reforestation along the headwaters of the southern drainage system than this catastrophe.

In the same manner no other public agency could have focused so much attention on curbing the age-old southern nemesis, forest fires. The Clarke-McNary law of 1924 had tremendously expanded the legislative mandate for national forest conservation, but its practical meaning depended on grass-roots community responses. The CCC contributed mightily to accomplishing the needed reversal of attitudes. It opened thousands of miles of woods access roads and trails and built fire towers across the region that quickly became as much sentinels of the new forest management as observation pinnacles for the detection and suppression of wild fires. Broad areas of southern timberlands were brought under systematic surveillance from these steel "country crow's nests." Coupled with the erection of the towers was the building of a widespread communications system in the form of hundreds of miles of telephone lines. In its ten-year existence in the South the CCC was occupied with an inordinate number of fire-fighting chores.

Aside from its more highly visible labors in the fields of soil conservation, reforestation, stand improvement, emergency work, and wildlife survey and protection, the corps had a lasting effect on myriad isolated pockets of Appalachia and the red-hill cotton South. It opened public roads in places where there had existed no more than dim foot and horse paths forming the most tenuous connections with the "outside." Many modern and heavily traveled secondary county and state roads were first opened by the CCC. Its labor force cleared rights-of-way, blasted roadbeds around steep mountain shoulders, erected directional signs, and otherwise reduced blighting isolation for thousands of landlocked people, allowing countrymen to gain for the first time in their family histories ready access to the world about them.

None of the reforestation and conservation efforts could have met with much success without the opening of roads and trails. The effectiveness of subsequent crusades against forest fires rested squarely upon the ability of protective agencies to penetrate threatened woodlands. In turn, successful marketing of forest products depended upon transportation. As vital as these facts were, it is historically reasonable to conclude that the accomplishment of greatest long-range significance was the CCC's development of highly visible demonstration practices of soil conservation and reforestation. These helped to change in a reasonably short time the ancient wasteful practices of mismanaging southern land and forest resources.

It is safe to assume that hundreds of thousands of southerners, born and raised in the pinewoods, had little or no knowledge of how their common trees were propagated beyond a vague notion that somehow or other old-field pines sprouted up in unusually thick clusters around the perimeters of abandoned fields, and that late every summer squirrels cut pine burrs. Most of them, perhaps, had never seen a pine seed, and had no idea in which month the seeds slipped out of the cones. Rural southerners learned many facts about trees by watching the CCC gather pine cones in October and shake the seed from them onto drying racks, later to be planted in nursery beds in the same way hillside farmers planted sweet potatoes and tobacco seeds.

Just as the CCC taught practical lessons of reforestation it achieved equally dramatic results in soil conservation. All-but-disbelieving patch farmer bystanders watched the corpsmen build catch-breaks across gullies and throw up terraces in sweeping contours around hillsides in order, as an East Tennessee mountaineer said, "to make the water walk instead of run downhill."

In the Tennessee Valley the CCC did the early and necessary ground work for the development of the remarkably successful Tennessee Valley Authority forestry program. On the barren hillsides the corpsmen initiated the soil conservation practices of the agency. The CCC introduced advances in soil and timber management that would be used to good purpose later. Nearly all of the southern states responded constructively to the demonstration lessons of the Civilian Conservation Corps by enacting more effective legislation, enlarging reforestation programs, creating tree nurseries, and recovering broad areas of submarginal lands that had seemed irretrievably spoiled.

Unhappily, entry of the United States into World War II brought dissolution of the CCC with its widely dispersed woodland camps. The war drew corpsmen away from the southern fields and forests for military duty; behind they left trails and roads unfinished, in some instances firetowers unmanned, and millions of trees and gullied acres unplanted. But after the end of the war the bright promise of the expansion of the papermaking industry in the South encouraged resumption of the forest conservation program where it was left off in June 1942 when the CCC was disbanded.

There still remain across the South stands of trees that were planted by the CCC, and on hundreds of thousands of acres there are monuments to the checking of soil erosion. Pinewoods are ridged with terraces laid off and built by corpsmen when the land was wasting away as abandoned cotton and tobacco fields. The fire towers that remain upright have become antique landmarks from the days of limited visual fire surveillance, but eloquently memorialize an era when public attitudes toward the place of soil and trees in the social and economic welfare of the South were sharply revised. Most dramatic of all, however, has been the miraculous reversal of southern land values and the bright promises of the region's capacity to nurture its basic and renewable resources.

7. The Tennessee Valley Experiment

There may never have been another time in the South's history, before or since 1933, when so many compromises as to land utilization and the conservation of resources could be made among governments, private landowners, and industries. Just as the chemical crisis of World War I had brought about the development of Muscle Shoals on the Tennessee River, the stifling depression of the early 1930s all but enforced common efforts at conservation.

Fortunately, the law creating the Tennessee Valley Authority gave its managers broad powers of direction and control. The mission of the Authority, freed of bureaucratic interference from Washington in areas of checking land wastage and controlling floods and fires, allowed prompt action. Beyond this was the broad problem of assuring industrial continuity by the nurturing and conserving of the sources of vital raw materials.

In 1929 an estimated 40 million acres of idle land existed in the South. This land was said to be wasting away each year at an increasing rate because of erosion and abandonment. The most important of the New Deal agencies, measured in scope of area covered, was the independent one created to bring about regional progress in the Tennessee Valley.

The central ganglia of the Tennessee River system penetrate parts of seven states and bear directly upon almost as many more. All of the system lies around the upper perimeter of the pine belt of the Atlantic coastal area and the lower South, yet much of the valley is covered in varying density with a variety of pines, including a generous amount of the scrubby Virginia shortleaf types. In no other part of the South is there a greater variety of commercial hardwoods, which once included giant American chestnut, a half dozen or more oaks, tulip poplar, swamp cypress, and tupelo gums. At the head of the valley is located the vast Pisgah National Forest, once part of the George Vanderbilt Estate, and a veritable large-scale forest laboratory for the study of Appalachian hardwoods.

On May 18, 1933, President Franklin D. Roosevelt signed the law creating the Tennessee Valley Authority, culminating a long and intricate political struggle. By a stroke of the presidential pen the historic old frontier region was set on a modern course to the future. The major sections of this law had far-reaching practical and philosophical importance to the region. The most important of these applied to flood control, the generation of electricity, the maintenance of open navigational channels, and general conservation of resources. The fourth and fifth sections of the law specifically instructed the directors of the newly created board to determine "the proper use of marginal lands and to select the best methods of reforestation." The sixth, or basically philosophical section, authorized a general search for the best means of assuring "the economic and social well-being of the people living in said river basin."

The creation of the Tennessee Valley Authority coincided with that of other New Deal agencies, especially the federal Soils Survey under the direction of Hugh H. Bennett, formerly of the Division of Soils of the Department of Agriculture, and the Emergency Conservation Works Program or Corps, later known as the CCC. The soils survey presented in broad outline the condition of the upper valley lands, thus creating a dependable base of knowledge upon which to make a valley-wide, intensive survey of the amount and state of marginal or abandoned lands. The Emergency Conservation Works Corps contributed material assistance to the upper stages of two of the TVA's congressional mandates.

In the area of reforestation the TVA was faced with the immediate task of making a resource inventory. This involved an unusually broad segment of public and private interests. At the outset it was somewhat handicapping that the United States Forest Service had been unable, for lack of money and manpower, to make a timber inventory. Too, the law creating the TVA failed to distinguish its responsibilities in the forestry area from those of the Forest Service. Later this oversight, if it was an oversight, was to create considerable differences of opinion as to the actual available timber resources of the valley. By 1950 it seemed clear that the TVA had much more complete and dependable data on the subject.

The drafting of a broad conservation program for a region as large and diverse as the Tennessee Valley confronted planners with complexities that neither advocates nor opponents of the law could foresee. First, the entire upper portion of the region lay in the path of the early westward movement, where folk mores were deeply imprinted upon the land. Pioneers who settled the country either brought to the Tennessee or quickly developed a pattern of life that proved destructive to timber and soil. Second, the Valley had since the second quarter of the nineteenth century been home to thousands of peckerwood sawmills and other small timber-using industries such as those described so eloquently in the *Foxfire* books.

Sawmill operators had greedily cutout the rich virgin timber stand with no thought of its depletion or of restoring it by reforestation. Finally, the concept of renewing the forest resource by planting trees as one would field crops had to be developed with patience and attention. This was especially true where subsistence farmers on marginal Appalachian lands had to depend upon diminishing annual harvests from their eroding fields. A farm demonstration agent told John W. Hershey, tree crop specialist for the Tennessee Valley Authority, in 1934: "Your tree crop idea sounds good to me. There is one thing sure, the farmers of this county need something. Their land is washing away and their situation is becoming desperate." Hershey said the idea of reforestation was new to most people of the valley. He visited over a hundred county agents in the process of making a preliminary survey of forest needs and conditions.

The timber cut in Tennessee had declined from 1.226 billion board feet in 1909 to 530 million feet in 1928. There were 2,644 sawmills in the state in the former year and 503 in the latter. G.H. Collingwood estimated in June, 1933, that with a proper combination of protection and management in the valley region the forest could easily produce an annual increment of 1.5 billion feet of commercial grade timber at the rate of 115 board feet on each of the estimated 13 million acres judged to be in reasonably acceptable growing condition.

In 1934, in a revised overview, foresters estimated there were 28 million acres of land in the Tennessee Valley area, one approximating the size of Pennsylvania. The new estimate of 18 million acres materially reduced the earlier area under some form of forest cover. This was to be explained largely because of a reconsideration of the nature of forest cover. Dealing with the same subject in 1944 in his book *Democracy on the March,* David Lilienthal wrote; "Fifty-four per cent of this valley is wooded, and of these 14 million wooded acres over 40 per belong to farmers." Whatever the precise forest acreage, there were more than a hundred species of commercial grade trees growing in the region, a fact that promised in time to become attractive to specialized wood-using industries. Fortunately for the TVA foresters at the outset of their survey there were in the region at least 4,600 Emergency Conservation Works men available who could be employed not only in an erosion control program but in the detailed forest survey and wood inventory. The Tennessee Valley Technical Forest Council was organized and was composed of representatives from the departments of forestry of the seven valley states. The Authority also received assistance from county agents and the extension service.

Soil exhaustion, the forest survey, and management were all of primary concern to TVA foresters, but none took precedence over fire control and the education of private landowners and their tradition-bound neighbors to the economic importance of their woods. With the excitement and drama of the comprehensive Tennessee Valley Program, farmers and timbermen alike were more easily appealed to for cooperation than had ever been true in southern history.

In 1933 the forest lands in the seven Tennessee Valley states were almost completly exposed to the ravages of wildfires. Even in areas where there was some semblance of organized protection it was highly inadequate. In 1934 the seven valley states appropriated less than half a million dollars to support their organized forestry programs, and their departments were staffed by only thirty-six foresters. The area burned over annually in the valley appears to have been in the neighborhood of a million acres, and much of this land had been burned over repeatedly. The valley was fairly well populated by habitual spring trash burners, malicious arsonists, and careless smokers, hunters, and campers. Also the highland portions of the region were especially subjected to fires started by lightning strikes on ridge top trees whose roots were grounded in the sandstone outcropping.

One of the first acts of the forestry division of the TVA was to organize an educational crusade to promote fire prevention and improved fire-fighting techniques, to teach the importance of timber management, and to advocate grazing practices compatible with the nature of the woodlands. The Authority produced motion pictures to illustrate the techniques of fire control. It made surveys to determine areas of high incidence of wood burnings, and the season in which men and machines had to be moved. The instructional programs were repeated often to drive home their messages. In a report covering the first two decades of operation of the TVA it was said there had been, between 1933 and 1947, 6,500 public demonstrations and meetings attended by 783,000 people. The Authority's foresters had visited areas of frequent fire occurrence to stress the importance of community-wide cooperation.

Officials in many valley counties cooperated in the organization of five-year plans in which they agreed to promote and give support to the modern forestry program through the county agents, local fire assessment tax programs, the enforcement of fire laws, and the use of public facilities for holding meetings. Such programs, involving more than 3 million acres of land, were organized in fifty counties in six of the seven states. The most impressive cooperation was said to have come from North Carolina's fifteen Tennessee Valley counties. They covered an area of 2.71 million acres on which the state's Department of Forestry and the TVA foresters agreed to sustain fire protection on both public and private lands, to explore the whole question of fire prevention, and to devise a working formula that could be applied in counties throughout the rest of the valley. The North Carolina experiment was said to have resulted in a phenomenal reduction in the number and scope of areas burned over by individual fires and in total acreage destroyed annually.

It may not have been altogether tragic that such a large proportion of valley lands were denuded of their original timber stand and that the soil was so impoverished. Maybe no other condition would have induced uninformed landholders to attend public assemblies in good numbers, to observe logging and timber demonstrations, and to accept the advice and direction of trained foresters so cooperatively. It took the combined excitement and fright of the depression, the broad-scale conservation work of the CCC, and the highly publicized planning of the entire interstate valley to win public commitment to reforestation.

The two Tennessee Valley Authority nurseries were able to supply enormous quantities of tree seedlings without cost to the landowner with which to plant marginal lands down to 1957. By 1968, and the date of closing the Clinton nursery, the TVA had supplied 603 million seedlings to be planted on private, TVA, and other federal lands. After the latter date corporate and state nurseries furnished seedlings, and by 1973, 1.3 million acres of land had been reforested since 1933.

The departments of forestry in the seven valley states increased their personnel from 36 in 1934 to 300 by 1952, and they increased expenditures from $500,000 to approximately $8 million. Not all this growth, of course, was due directly to the impact of the TVA; it would be impossible to separate the effects of TVA activities from those of independent state and corporate efforts in reforestation.

An era came to an end in TVA history in 1960 when the two public nurseries were closed. The Clinton nursery site was converted to an industrial area. The seven states had developed their own nurseries, which could fill the needs of most private landowners and publicly-owned lands, and the larger wood products industries had established company nurseries that furnished seedlings for corporate lands and for many private landowners.

In addition to the nursery developments, the TVA foresters later experimented with the process of direct seeding. Using a tractor planter, which operated on the same principle as mechanical agricultural planters, tree seeds were deposited directly in the ground where it was hoped they would form sufficient contact with the mineral earth to germinate. In 1963, 3,120 acres were planted in this manner. Beginning in 1964 TVA and local forest agencies began experimenting with direct seeding of Virginia and loblolly pines in selected strip-mined areas. Three seeded areas sprouted from 1,200 to 1,600 plants per acre, perhaps three times as many stems as should be allowed to stand for maximum production. Generally the direct seeding experiments were successful, especially where fertilizers were applied after the seedlings were a year old.

When the Forestry Division of TVA abandoned seedling production it turned to other areas of research. In 1971 it embarked upon a program in forest genetics in which seed, especially from oaks and tulip poplar, were sought for gathering from superior trees. A year later foresters reported having gathered enough seed stock to produce 50,000 seedlings from 229 "superior" or average northern red oaks. A process of controlled pollination was used in making a hundred crosses on a thousand individual poplar flowers. In earlier years the division had experimented with the selection and production of superior pines, but after 1970 it left this popular field to state and corporate forestry departments. A major difficulty in establishing the new forest in the Tennessee Valley is that so much native growth is either of inferior quality or outright trash. To reverse this condition takes time, money, and infinite patience. Research in forest genetics is controlled largely by nature's own timetable, and in the case of the valley hardwoods it takes a scientist two or three decades to determine definitely the success or failure in cross-breeding. The only short-range check the tree geneticist has is the rate of early growth and foliage appearance and conformation.

It was not the objective of the great forestry campaign of 1930-1960 to supply timber to enable the valley peckerwood sawmills to begin all over again the raping of the woods. In order to carry out the congressional mandate of 1933 it was necessary for the public foresters to assure a continuous supply of wood to a permanently located industrial complex within a reasonable distance from the source of supply. Before 1933 no major capital industry had located in the Tennessee Valley, with the possible exception of a few large sawmills in the Nashville and Huntsville areas, and the Champion Fibre Company at Canton on the upper Pigeon River in North Carolina. Control of soil erosion and the instigation of reforestation were basic to the success of the extensive valley experiments, as were flood control and the generation of electrical current; these aims, however, did not necessarily serve the immediate needs of much of the valley population. To provide personal and corporate income and sustain businesses, towns, cities, local governments, and public institutions would require the importation of new and more modern industries and the creation of regional pools of capital. One of the most exciting industrial chapters in the history of the TVA was the location of the Bowater Southern Paper Corporation's newsprint mill in 1952 at Calhoun on the Hiwassee River.

In 1943, when southern newspaper publishers were desperately in need of a new source of newsprint, TVA issued a report entitled *Factual Data for Use as a Basis for Determining the Practicality of Establishing a Pine Pulp Mill in the Tennessee Valley—Analysis of Possible Sites.* This publication reached Silliman Evans, publisher of the *Nashville Tennesseean,* who sent it on to Sir Eric Bowater in London. At the time Bowater executives were searching for a site on which to establish a newsprint mill either in the United States or Canada. Sites were examined in the Northwestern states and in the Pacific provinces of Canada. Evans encouraged TVA chairman David Lilienthal to meet with Bowater representatives in his office in Nashville in June 1944. A.B. Meyer, president of the American Bowater affiliate, was present. Two months later the paper company officials met with "five high executives" of the state and TVA in the Washington office of the Authority, but soon thereafter, so far as anybody in East Tennessee knew, Bowater gave up the idea of coming either to the United States or to the South.

After a silence of almost seven years the Bowater site location team again became active. In the first half of 1951 it cruised the Tennessee Valley and tentatively selected two locations, one at Naheola, Alabama, and the other at the village of Calhoun, Tennessee, on the Hiwassee River. The Bowater men were said to have cruised the area continuously for six months. A.W. Bentley, the company's forestry consultant, repeatedly visited the various forestry installations of the TVA, so frequently in fact that the Authority's foresters dubbed his visitations the "Bowater Trail." The Bowater site cruisers were discriminating in their survey "The end of the long trail appeared," said Roscoe C. Martin, "when the Bowater survey group visited a site which lay along the Hiwassee River at Calhoun, in East Tennessee. This was the last of the prospective locations to be visited by the group, which having inspected 21 southern sites before, came to the Calhoun site at the end of what was to prove their last inspection trip." Perhaps this site had been one of several suggested by the J.E. Sirrine Company, locational engineers of Greenville, South Carolina, or it may have been a desperation suggestion by officials of TVA.

The spot beside the enlarged embayment of the Hiwassee had an almost instant appeal for the Bowater officials. It was said that Arthur Baker, leader of the site inspectors, rushed up to the top of a knoll on the site and proclaimed in Brigham Young fashion, "This is the place." Here was ready access to the main line of the Southern Railway between Knoxville and Chattanooga, to Highway 11, and to navigation on the Tennessee River system. Also available was an all but inexhaustible supply of superb quality industrial water—a supply many times over Bowater's demand for 25 million gallons a day. TVA could supply sufficient electrical power to supplement company-generated electricity, and the trunkline of the East Tennessee Natural Gas Company ran through the proposed site. In addition, there was the 1,800 acres of land deemed necessary for a major paper mill. Beyond these physical necessities there was promise of an adequate local labor force with which to carry on both mill and wood supply operations.

Obviously the primary need of a paper mill is a constantly renewable supply of wood, principally pine. In the case of the projected Bowater mill this meant approximately 3 million standard cords of pulpwood a year. A.B. Meyer asked Gordon Clapp, chairman of the TVA Board of Directors, if the mill could "safely count on procuring this amount of pulpwood out of the Tennessee Valley, northern Georgia, and northern Alabama on a permanent basis without overcutting the forest areas and without interfering with the pulpwood supplies of mills that are already established and draw pulpwood from these same areas?" This request opened a somewhat vigorous discussion between the staff of TVA Division of Forestry and the United States Forest Service spokesmen, a dispute caused largely by differences between the two services in the making of stand appraisals. Discrepancies arose because Forest Service data were generalized and failed to take full account of the potential of the newly planted areas in the valley.

In 1951, pine plantations established in the 1930s by the CCC had only entered the preliminary stages of maturity, and TVA foresters did not have enough data to make a reasonable statement of the quantity of wood they would eventually produce. It was evident, however, that they had a more detailed notion of the forest potential than did the Forest Service. In fairness it must be said the latter service operated on a much broader scale of forest management.

The situation was further complicated when Bowater filed, May 25, 1951, an application seeking a certificate of necessity from the National Defense Administration. Between this date and February 19, 1952, occurred a complicated series of conferences, disputes among foresters, bureaucratic delays, exertions of political pressure, and opposition from the Mead Corporation and the Champion Fibre Company. Mead had recently located a kraft mill at Rome, Georgia, on the southern extremity of the proposed Bowater acquisition territory, and Champion operated its half-century-old paper mill on the east at Canton, North Carolina. Champion had entered the South at the beginning of the new paper age and had acquired in the neighborhood of a quarter of a million acres of timberland. Both companies expressed fear that Bowater would compete heavily for wood. Reuben B. Robertson, Jr., president of Champion, wrote Charles Sawyer, secretary of commerce, in September, 1951, protesting that the substantial drain of Bowater on the existing timber resources would further deplete an already limited supply of pulpwood. A month later the Mead Company published an analysis of the pine pulpwood situation in the Tennessee Valley in which it said that East Tennessee was primarily a hardwood producing area and that there was not sufficient pine pulpwood to sustain the operation of three mills. Like the Forest Service, the two companies seemed to overlook the conservation and reforestation accomplishments of the Forestry Division of the TVA.

Conflict between the established paper companies and the TVA Division of Forestry was time consuming and in the end appears to have been entirely futile. Rumors were started that the Bowater mill would supply British customers only, which would mean shipping out of the country newsprint needed by southern publishers. It was said the company would employ only British executives, engineers, technicians, and even common laborers in the construction and operation of the mill.

Under the leadership of Charles Tebbe, the United States Forest Service was advisor to the National Defense Administration on matters pertaining to the availability of timber supplies.

Tebbe and the Forest Service contended that the new mill should be located in one of twenty-nine western Virginia and North Carolina counties that had surplus pine pulpwood. On August 16, 1951, Charles Tebbe and his colleague H.R. Josephson conferred with A.B. Meyer and the company's Washington attorney Arthur J. Swanick. Tebbe had actually prepared a memorandum disapproving the issuance of the certificate of necessity to Bowater for the Calhoun site. Bowater officials were firm in their commitment to the Calhoun location. After long and sometimes vigorous arguments had rocked back and forth between TVA foresters and those of the Forest Service, and after an impressive amount of press, business, labor, and political pressure, a certificate of necessity was issued the company without either amendments or restrictions on wood procurement on February 19, 1952.

With the granting of the certificate, Bowater Southern Paper Corporation was left free to build its Calhoun mill, to purchase timberlands, and to acquire wood wherever it was available in the valley. The twenty-nine Virginia-North Carolina counties were considered a surplus growth area from which the company could procure wood if other sources were threatened with over-cutting. By this authorization Bowaters was spared the added expense of a 350-mile rail haul from the remote counties.

The newsprint mill on the Hiwassee was two years in building. In the meantime the Hiwassee Land Company, a Bowater Southern subsidiary, purchased timberlands, located a tree nursery, and joined the Tennessee Valley Authority in the eternal crusade to prevent and suppress fires and promote reforestation.

For the first time in valley history a major wood-using industry had located there. It was an occasion of considerable historic and economic importance when the *Atlanta Journal*, August 4, 1954, published an edition on Bowaters newsprint. Within a few weeks the $60-million Calhoun mill supplied paper to 184 newspapers in fifteen southern and neighboring states. Earlier the Knoxville *News-Sentinel* published a feature story in which the paper said two-thirds of its newsprint had until then come from Maine and Canada. It now had contracted to take 5,000 tons annually from the downriver Calhoun mill. At no time did the Bowater Southern mill exhaust its wood supply or threaten East Tennessee and neighboring forests with overharvesting.

Eight years after the first newsprint came from the Calhoun plant, the Tennessee Valley Authority was in a position to publish an analysis of its work in reclamation of submarginal land and in reforestation. Its Division of Forestry reported in 1962 that it has supplied 483.5 million seedlings to plant 80,000 acres of public lands, and to 85,700 private plantations totaling 494,000 acres. Most of the plantings were made in old fields either abandoned or badly depleted by erosion. Almost miraculously, 98 percent of the free seedlings of the agency's nurseries were put in the ground. Plantations ranged from less than ten to 750 acres. By 1970 TVA reported that 21.6 million acres of the Tennessee Valley were under forest cover; during the decade 1960-1970 wood volume had increased from 300 million to 329 million cubic feet, leaving a margin of standing and growing timber of almost 16 billion feet.

When Congress enacted the Tennessee Valley Authority law in May 1933, none of its supporters could have anticipated the changes that would come about in the agency's functions and within the region it was to serve. Emphasis in 1933 was upon the production of electrical energy by utilization of the Tennessee River system stream flow. By 1940 TVA was moving rapidly into the field of steam-generated electricity.

Ironically, the coal industry opposed TVA down into the late 1940s, pretending to believe that the hydroelectric plants would rob coal producers of a large part of their valley market. In the early war years TVA purchased 5.5 million tons of coal, with the tonnage doubling each year. After 1940 there was major expansion of steam plants. All of this was unforeseen in the early 1930s. Too, no one could have anticipated the rise of new coal-mining technology, involving the stripping off of earth by monstrous shovels and extraction of coal by giant augers. This in time would involve the Tennessee Valley Authority, both within its watershed area and in the outlying territories of its contracting coal suppliers.

World War II stimulated enormous demands for electrical energy by the new industries that moved into the valley. After 1960 the wood using industries made additional heavy demands on the TVA for energy, and so did the rapidly expanding urban communities within the area. The consumption of coal rose in proportion, a large portion of it coming from stripped lands. So far as anyone knew in 1950 the stripped and abandoned minefields could never be reclaimed by natural processes, and there was no appreciable knowledge of methods by which a forest cover could be restored. Restoration of contour and productive soil conditions was a costly undertaking, ranging from $50 to $2,000 an acre.

The TVA was involved in the strip-mining controversy on two sides—as a major consumer of coal in its steam-fired plants, and by its commitment to the restoration and conservation of the land. Environmentalist groups attacked the agency in March 1971 with the charge that it was following a policy of land and forest management inconsistent with one of its mandates of 1933. Three environmentalist organizations filed suit against the agency that month in the Second United States Circuit Court, charging that TVA was in violation of the National Environmental Policy Act of 1969. They sought to enjoin the Authority from purchasing coal from strip miners. In 1972 the Court ruled TVA was not in violation, and permitted the agency to proceed with its purchases and application of its strip-mine policies. That year TVA had entered into contracts to purchase 29,864 million tons of coal from Alabama, Illinois, Kentucky, Tennessee, and Virginia mines for $6 million. Half of this would come from deep mines. It was estimated that in filling these contracts 31,000 acres of land would be disturbed. "Left to nature," said the TVA scientists, "it will be many years before these gullied strips can again take their proper place in the region's ecology." The Authority proposed to cooperate with state and local governments in reclaiming 70,000 acres.

TVA in 1965 included a reclamation of strip-mined land in its coal contracts and initiated a program for dealing with the sterilized areas, many of which were stripped before the coal states adopted reclamation laws. In making its large annual purchases of coal TVA obviously had a heavy impact upon the fate of the land. A good example of the highly visible and ghastly ravages of strip mining was the area surrounding the Paradise Island steam plant in eastern Muhlenburg County, Kentucky. Huge shovels scooped millions of tons of soil overburden from the coal seam, destroying the forest cover and leaving behind a scene of desolation comparable to the lunar surface. Fortunately the problem of restoring the land to approximately its original contour was less difficult there than in Appalachian eastern Kentucky and Tennessee. Whether or not a forest cover comparable to the one destroyed can be regrown remains to be seen, however.

TVA, either out of commitment to the conservation of the land of the valley and its natural resources or in response to the sting of public criticism, published in its annual report for 1972 an eloquent statement: "In broadest terms, the overriding issue in the years just ahead will continue to be the frustratingly complex effort to balance the twin goals of economic growth and environmental quality. The key word is 'balance.' A pristine environment has little meaning for a jobless man whose family is hungry, just as material affluence is useless if, in creating it, we continue to foul the earth." Reclamation standards in its restrictive coal purchase contracts TVA said were intended in part as a demonstration of desirable practices, to nudge the states into enacting needed laws and regulations.

For every million tons of coal lifted from a stripped seam, a significant forest potential was thwarted if not destroyed. By 1971, TVA reported that it had brought about the reconditioning and planting of 2,500 acres of spoil lands in four test strip-mine areas.

In the 1940s before strip-mining coal and wholesale land disturbance occurred, the TVA had encountered the problem of land restoration on the sites of its phosphate mines in Middle Tennessee with moderate results; the Authority was able to transfer knowledge of its experience from this area to the stripped coal regions. It conducted surveys of barren mine deserts, sought to stimulate public reaction, and sought the enactment of strict regulatory laws in Kentucky, Alabama, and Tennessee beginning in 1945. Kentucky adopted a basic strip mine law in 1954 and nearly every succeeding General Assembly has amended it. Virginia passed a regulatory strip mine law in 1966. In Kentucky owners of forest lands, but not of the mineral rights beneath them, were left defenseless in the protection of their timber stands because of the infamous "broad form deed" which gave the mineral rights owner priority in the use of the land. Because of this cancerous legality thousands of acres of Kentucky timberlands have been destroyed, and it is from some of these lands that TVA has purchased much of its coal.

By 1974 the strip miners in five coal states had reconditioned 10,225 acres of surface-mined land. In a revision of its original policy TVA required prospective suppliers of coal to present restoration plans before they submitted bids. This procedure was somewhat simplified as several of the states strengthened their surface mine laws. TVA conducted demonstrations of surface mining procedures and land reclamation in Campbell County, Tennessee, and on a site in Morgan County just north of Oakdale. Working with the coal contractor TVA scientists sought to develop procedures for constructing silt basins, burying toxic materials, and replacing top soil. Possibly these experiments have not had time to give clear indications as to the long-term effects of such drastic disturbances of the land on the potential for a productive forest cover.

The construction of Kentucky Dam on the Tennessee River and Barkley Dam on the Cumberland brought a sharp revision of the historic area long called by the native population "land between the rivers." North of state highway 79 in Tennessee, skirting around the town of Dover, and south of the dams lies a ridge of hickory-oak forest-farm lands of approximately 170,000 acres. This area, with a mixed history of farming, iron mining, lumbering, moonshining, and mussel fishing, was occupied in June 1963 by 950 families numbering 2,700 people. When President Kennedy signed the law in 1963 creating a national recreational area to be called officially "The Land Between the Lakes," it was turned over to the TVA to be developed and managed. One of the major problems of forest management in the Tennessee Valley has long been that of producing a high quality hardwood timber supply, and the Land Between the Lakes is almost an ideal area for extensive experimentation and improvement in the growing of improved hardwoods.

Perhaps no other occasion has arisen in the eastern part of the nation where so many Anglo-American people had to be moved from their long established homes. In the Land Between the Lakes historical and sentimental ties had been developed in the century and a half since the Jackson Purchase was added to Kentucky and Tennessee in 1818. Churches, homes, and businesses were uprooted, and family cemeteries became isolated in woodlands. To date the Tennessee Valley Authority has lacked the necessary funds to develop and maintain fully the many recreational sites available to it in this picturesque strip of forest land. Nevertheless the land with its growing timber remains intact and is managed as an important addition to the timbered domain of the South.

It would be difficult if not impossible to differentiate the influence of the Tennessee Valley Authority, 1933-1984, from the economic expansion and improvements that would have occurred in the course of changing times. In the field of forest management revolutionary changes occurred throughout the rest of the South, and no doubt many of these were profoundly influenced by what occurred in the Tennessee Valley heartland. Nevertheless the accomplishments of the Authority can be measured in terms of hundreds of demonstration tree plantations, the offering of instruction in the techniques of management and stand preservation, the organization of two large nurseries, a continuing forest research program, and the stimulation of the seven valley states to enlarge the services of their departments of forestry and to assume responsibility for instituting modern forest management. Beyond these accomplishments, it may be that TVA's most important contribution was the demonstration that wood-using industries in the valley could locate on permanent sites and carry on continuous operations.

In 1975 the Tennessee Valley Authority published its fifth and most comprehensive five-year analysis of forest statistics. It said that there were 21.6 million acres of forest land, which supported a billion-dollar wood-using industry. This meant that three-fifths of the Tennessee Valley was under forest cover. The latter acreage estimate was up from the 18-million-acre estimate in 1934, and was based on a total area of 36.5 million acres in the 125 counties of the valley. Significantly, the forest area had been reduced by 173,000 acres since

1933 by the creation of new lakes and streamside sterile areas; the lake water surface area alone was increased by 64,000 acres. The volume of growing timber, however, had increased in five years from 21.2 billion to 24.7 billion cubic feet, and was judged to be increasing at the rate of 3.33 percent annually. Valley forested areas were estimated to contain, by international log scale measurement, nearly 61 billion board feet, or an average of 4,378 board feet per acre.

Through the generation of abundant electrical power and the control of soil erosion, silting, and flooding in most of the 125-county area, the TVA over the years has helped to create conditions conducive to urban growth and industrial expansion, and thereby helped to reduce the area of commerical forest lands available. On the other hand, its reservoir areas have become managed forests and they increase materially the wood-using potential. In January 1984, Tennessee was reported to have lost a million acres of forest lands to newly cleared farms and urban expansion. Control of both hardwood and pinelands was still in the hands of private owners, "But," said Karl Wolfshohl of the *Progressive Farmer*, "Good timber management is scarce, and the quality of hardwood timber continues to decline."

In 1944 David Lilienthal wrote with evident exuberance, "The plentiful rainfall and long growing season in the valley push trees along at an incredible rate. From where I write I can see a slope that nine years ago was newly planted with pine seedlings; today most of the trees are eighteen to twenty-five feet tall, and the hillside is a dense green bank. In private woodland forest, on thousands of acres of TVA reservoir land, the forests of the valley are coming back." His successors have written less eloquently on the subject, but with impressive practicality in terms of paper mills and other wood-using industries located in the valley, and with trees enough growing in the woods to keep them operating. The rate of employment, a billion-dollar industrial growth, and smokeless Indian summers and falls further document the impact the TVA has had upon the heartland of the timber-producing South. Even so, perhaps only two-thirds of the Tennessee Valley's real timber productive potential has been realized in both management and harvesting procedures. Loggers still leave a large volume of hardwood trees behind to rot in their bed for a lack of demand for this type of wood.

8. Charles Herty's Legacy

Slowly but certainly the application of chemistry in industry brought about a revolution in many phases of southern economic life, and especially in the management of the South's second and third forests. During the crucial post–World War I years, 1920-1936, scientists began looking at southern woods from a new perspective. In the early twenties lumbering had been sharply reduced, southern farming generally was in a state of doldrums, and vast areas of submarginal cotton lands were being reclaimed by old-field pines and trash shrubbery. The wood harvesting industry, like southern farming, lacked diversity. Though the art of manufacturing kraft paper was well known in the South, that industry was narrowly limited to the production of coarse shopping and grocery bags, industrial papers, cardboard boxing, and packing materials.

Down to 1922 no scientist had with certainty broken through the resin barrier in the production of white paper and newsprint in industrial quantities from pine pulp. In fact, scientists and mill operators had only limited knowledge of the full relationship of pine resin and wood fiber. At Hartsville, South Carolina, the Cokers had experienced what seemed almost insoluble difficulties in the production of kraft papers in their Carolina Fibre Mill. It was only by trial and error that they finally succeeded.

The United States in 1930 consumed paper products manufactured from approximately 12 million cords of pulpwood; 70 percent of this relatively large volume was imported from Canada and other countries. This amounted to an annual consumption of approximately 8.5 million cords of foreign wood, and at a time when more than 100 million acres of poor southern lands were said to be capable under proper management of producing 150 million cords of pulpwood.

The South's future, however foggy it was in 1920, depended on how intelligently its leaders understood the imperatives of change. It was further estimated that the South still had intact nearly 224 billion board feet of timber in varying stages of maturity and quality. There remained a rich pool of potential wealth in the southern forest if only chemists could fathom the mysteries of converting raw wood into processed products. This could be accomplished only if chemical means could be found to neutralize resin in all the pine stocks, but especially in the heart portions of the plentiful slash pine. Although the half dozen or so kraft mills operating in the South in 1930 produced approximately 3 million tons of sulphite pulp, and had largely assumed the national lead in the production of coarse kraft products, they by no means had begun to realize the full potential of the pine pulp paper industry.

As early as 1922 an experiment had succeeded in the making of bleached newsprint on test machines at 75 feet roll-off per minute. But to produce a profit a 200-inch wide roll had to come from the papermaking machine at a speed of 1000 feet per minute. In that same year, Warren B. Bullock of New York wrote in the *Manufacturers Record* that "there seems to be no reason to doubt that American ingenuity will eventually find a way of removing the pitch and rosin which is the greatest handicap at present to the making of sulphite paper from southern woods." But the problem was to resist solution for another decade.

The shortleaf pine, or *Pinus echinata*, forms a rich and heavily impregnated heart wood, which made it unsuitable for pulping by earlier processes. This particular pine was known by various names in different parts of the South. In the Atlantic rim it was called Cuban pine; in the hill southland it was known as old-growth shortleaf. Chemists working in the Forest Products Laboratory in Madison, Wisconsin, discovered that loblolly or *Pinus taeda*, the old-field type associated with abandoned fields and some cutover lands, and longleaf pines in the first quarter of a century of their growth presented fewer problems. All the southern pines, however, required special and as yet undiscovered methods of treatment.

The forest laboratory had conducted the necessary preliminary research on southern pinewoods and had defined many of the problems connected with the bleaching of each of the three types of southern pulp. The scientists in Wisconsin had also ground several other varieties of southern woods to test fiber strengths, color, and responses to the application of chemicals. At an early stage they had produced a light fawn shade of kraft paper from the three pine samples under laboratory conditions. What had not been determined was whether or not a reasonably inexpensive process for cooking large and continuous quantities of pulpwood could be accomplished in commercial runs in kraft mills.

In making the experiments in Madison a shipment of ordinary old-field loblolly pine logs was sent up from South Carolina. These were stored for periods ranging from two to four years before they were chipped. By the time these logs were readied for pulping they had become deeply stained with blue mold. Nevertheless, from these samples the Forest Products Laboratory produced specimens of white writing paper comparable to commercial grades then being sold in stationery stores. Also, papers of high quality were produced when other fibers were mixed with the southern pine pulp. A further experiment demonstrated that a commerical grade of grease-proof paper could be manufactured. Director Winslow said he saw in the test results promise that an almost unlimited expansion of the paper industry in the South could be based upon the fiber of the loblolly "weed" tree alone. He was certain the laboratory study "opens up the possibility of a 'two industry' forest—logs for lumber; tops, thinnings and other waste for pulp."

The laboratory experiments only pointed the way to use of the sulphate process for reducing pine chips to soft light fibers. Production of commercial white paper and newsprint in large quantities from the three species of pine pulp awaited further chemical and mechanical experimentation and refinement by chemists and engineers in a simulated papermill operation.

One of the most influential personalities of this era was Charles Holmes Herty of Savannah, Georgia, who had earlier developed the "Herty cup" for the turpentine industry. From his early days as a professor of chemistry in the University of North Carolina, Herty had contended that the pine tree could become the source of economic redemption for the South. He was convinced that pine pulp could be converted into commercial white paper, newsprint, and rayon fiber. An excellent publicist, he spread this doctrine in scientific papers and in speeches across the South. He was ready to speak to any group that would sit and listen—businessmen, farmers, lumbermen, editors, and legislators. To these he preached the use of knowledge already gained from the expanding kraft paper industry to promote wider diversification of uses for forest products. With other chemists and industrialists, he campaigned vigorously for the support of a scientific search for a formula for the making of white paper from resinous southern pine stock.

These efforts bore fruit early in 1932. Despite the blighting depression of the time, excitement had begun to run high in the southern paper industry. National demand for domestic paper products was rising and a well publicized depletion of northern pulpwood resources had driven up prices. At the same time there was a significant labor cost differential between northern and southern pulpwood. The Southern Kraft Corporation, a subsidiary of the International Paper Company, had just completed a $10-million mill at Panama City, Florida; the Brown Paper Company of Maine had made a $5-million addition to its pioneer plant, and the Champion Fibre Company was enlarging its Canton, North Carolina plant. Thus the support Herty sought was forthcoming for a new laboratory that would also be a simulated paper mill.

The Chemical Foundation, Incorporated, contributed $50,000 toward the construction of the experimental mill in Savannah. The Georgia legislature supplemented this fund in 1932 and 1933 with an appropriation of $40,000 to finance operation of the laboratory. Remaining costs of the plant were borne by the Savannah Industrial Committee, the kraft industry, the Central of Georgia Railroad Company, and the Savannah Electric and Power Company.

Herty, who not long before had been appointed research chemist for the Georgia Department of Forestry and Geological Development, was placed in charge of the experimental plant. Although his immediate goal was to discover a dependable process of producing white paper, he hoped to make possible the milling of an adequate supply of newsprint to free southern newspaper publishers from dependence on imported papers. Actually, his interest reached well beyond this objective to the reclamation of southern timberlands, and finding a way to establish a more profitable economic base for the cotton-jaded South.

The Savannah scientist had the advantage of a fund of knowledge derived from the trials and tribulations of papermaking from pine pulp in the past. James Lide Coker's vexatious experiences with the resinous pine pulp in his South Carolina Fibre Company pioneering plant, 1891-1895, had made vital contributions. Other southern

kraft papermakers had accumulated useful knowledge of the techniques of grinding and reducing pinewood to pulp and of converting
pulp into coarse paper and cardboard.

The big challenge facing the Savannah laboratory in 1932 was not
the elementary one of manufacturing paper, but of finding a chemical
bleaching formula that would neutralize the resin content of all pinewoods, so that paper of uniform quality could be manufactured on a
large scale at costs low enough to compete with the products of
northern and Canadian papermakers. One of the remarkable facts
about the Herty laboratory was that the staff was able to answer the
rudimentary questions in such a short time.

Associated with Herty in the laboratory-mill were G.C. Naugh-
ton, formerly of the Forest Products Laboratory, and then employed
by the George H. Mead Paper Company; Bruce Suttle, an experienced papermaker; W. Allen, a chemist formerly with the Pan-American
Petroleum Company; and J.B. Allen, an oil and sugar chemist. By
June of the first year of operation Herty announced that the research
pulp and paper mill was in operation. It had already been determined by James Lide Coker earlier and by the Forest Products Laboratory that the young southern pines contained no higher resin content during the first quarter of a century of growth than northern
spruce. Pulp from these native southern stocks could be successfully
processed either by sulphate or mechanical procedures.

From the outset the Savannah experimenters produced a good
grade of white paper. Their continuing investigations dealt with several varieties of wood, and sought to discover as many shortcuts as
possible for the manufacture of white and newsprint papers in large
commercial quantities. From newsprint created in Savannah, Herty
was able to persuade a southern newspaper publisher to print a special edition, and thus to begin a new era for southern and American
newspaper publishing.

A lead editorial in the *Manufacturers Record*, July 7, 1932, was ec-
static about the Herty findings:

> Laboratory tests had indicated that fine white paper and
> newsprint could be made from slash pine, but the announce-
> ment by Charles H. Herty, director of the experimental paper
> plant at Savannah, that these products also had been suc-
> cessfully made from longleaf and loblolly pines of the South
> is of the utmost significance. The definite known results of

this research work open a great opportunity for the South. These later developments of Dr. Herty and his associates are more far-reaching than the first successful endeavor to make white paper from slash pine for they make apparent at once the huge available supply of pulp wood.

These were prophetic views. It might not have been too extravagant in 1932 to boast that the Savannah staff had equalled the achievement of Eli Whitney in providing the technological basis for long-range southern economic growth, without involving all the biting social problems associated with the cotton gin and a staple crop.

Charles H. Herty neither claimed nor can be given sole credit for the breakthrough in neutralizing resins and in developing processes for reducing southern soft and hardwoods into pulp and then webbing them into commercial grade papers. He must, however, be credited with the vision and the fervent missionary preachments that a great abundance of newsprint could be manufactured from pines grown on lands formerly written off. He crusaded for the development of the newsprint industry in the depths of the Great Depression, and in a period when shortsighted and conservative editors were debating in their associations the possible effects of radio on their papers.

The year before the Savannah experimental plant was in operation Herty made as provocative speech as any in the history of the South. Speaking before the Southern Newspaper Association in the Grove Park Inn in Asheville, North Carolina, he told the audience of editors and managers that, "Mills in Canada and New England have to carry some 350,000 acres of land to maintain a perpetual supply of pulpwood for a 100-ton mill. . . . in the South you can run on one tenth that amount or 35,000 acres. With more sunlight we can make as much wood in a year on 35,000 acres as can be made on 350,000 acres in a cooler climate. That is the blessing of the South. That is what sunlight means to us." In that meeting he displayed samples of creamy sulphite pulp made from southern pine stock, and proclaimed it "as pretty a pulp as was ever seen."

Herty advised the southern editors to join in a cooperative venture to supply their demand for newsprint from native woods. He appeared to be convinced that it was now only a matter of months until the scientists in Savannah would be able to perfect the techniques of reducing southern pine pulp to large-volume newsprint production. This faith received further confirmation when the Beaver Wood Fibre Company, Ltd. of Thorold, Ontario, produced Savannah pulp into newsprint at the rate of 715 feet per minute without a break. In November 1933 nine daily southern papers printed editions on this paper.

But Herty died before he saw the full realization of his prophecy. It was not until 1940 that the first newsprint in commercial quantity came from the Southland Paper Mill near Lufkin, Texas. In quick succession the other companies came into the South. The English Bowater Southern Paper Company transferred its operations from Corner Brook, Newfoundland, to Calhoun, Tennessee. The International Paper Company produced its first newsprint in its Mobile plant and the following year placed its Pine Bluff, Arkansas, mill in operation. By 1960 the roll of paper mills located in the South had begun to represent a considerable roster of the industry. Such famous paper mills as Champion Fibre, Mead Paper, St. Regis, West Virginia Paper and Pulp, International Paper, Union Bag-Camp, Scott, Brown, Bowaters, and Buckeye Paper were in operation, and in time other companies joined the parade.

By no means had all the technical and operational problems of manufacturing white paper from the southern woods been resolved at Savannah. These were dealt with in day-to-day operations. What had happened at Savannah was removal of doubt that the second forest products industry could thrive in the South.

By 1933 the major challenges of the lumber and paper industries lay beyond the walls of the laboratories and the mills. The South, though not without appreciable remaining stands of log and lumber resources, was certain to approach a period, if past conditions prevailed, when this resource would be dangerously exhausted. The whole process of harvesting and management had to be placed under review, and that ancient and soul-wearying scourge, wild fire, had to be brought under control. Like some ancient people bewailing their tragedies at a sacred wailing wall, informed southerners cried out in print, in open forum, and in private against the wanton arsonists who persistently burned much of the region into deeper poverty. It was a hazardous business to build a costly enterprise dependent upon a resource that could be seriously injured or destroyed overnight in a woods fire.

Actually, most of the second forest was only about halfway to maturity, and its promise could still not be fully assessed. Landowners were so badly discouraged by the weakening of traditional staple-crop culture that they had not even begun to adjust emotionally to the surrender of large areas of their lands to the new nonagricultural crop. If farmers on the land were in confusion, legislators in the statehouses were even more perplexed. A new industry of the proportions and implications of the new paper mills could not come into the region and begin permanent operation without state laws being repealed or revised and new ones enacted. For instance, it was necessary in time to enact tax laws that levied a fire protection assessment on each acre of timberland.

At the time the heartening news came from Savannah, the depressed South stood in urgent need of grassroots education to convince its potential tree farmers of the importance of creating a revenue-producing second forest on abandoned farms and cutover lands. It was necessary to overcome an ingrained folk disregard, if not outright antagonism, toward the lowly pine tree, and especially the trifling loblolly that pushed its head up as an almost indestructible living testimonial of poverty and economic defeat, to develop popular and financial support for research into techniques of reforestation and land management, and to disseminate the information, written in the simplest and most practical forms possible, to farmers and landholders. It was also necessary to create state and industrial tree nurseries of sufficient capacity to supply a rising demand for planting stock.

Even at the outset of the New Deal years forested areas were shrinking because of the clearing of new grounds and pastures, the expansion of roads, the growth of towns and cities, the opening of modern power line rights-of-way, and rural-commercial preemptions of land. There was no lack of statistics on these changes; in fact the forest industry was all but drowned in statistics, most of which were to be proved inadequate by later and more efficient surveys. Actually it was not known in 1930 how many acres of land still remained under forest cover in the South, despite what the census of that year reported. But enough facts were available to show that the lumber industry in earlier years had cut deeply, if not nearly disastrously, into the original stands of timber, that forest fires had denuded approximately 30 million acres of pinelands alone, and that if the South was to sustain a rising demand for wood by the new industries it would have to conduct a vigorous program of replanting and modern management to the vacant lands in all the states.

After 1933 and the introduction of the Herty process of manufacturing white paper and newsprint, there was a need for dependable data as to how much southern land could be profitably converted to the growing of pulpwood, the growth characteristics of the major pine species under varying conditions, the reproductive span of hardwoods, and the most efficient harvesting procedures. The contention that trees could become as much a crop for southern farmers as cotton, corn, and sugar cane had to be demonstrated in practice. Possibly the most difficult barrier of all was the time span required for even the most minimal growth for commercial sale. Few forest owners had practiced the marking of trees, selective cutting, or staggered sales so as to sustain a continuing income from tree farming. The Southern Pine Association, founded in 1914, began promoting the American Tree Farm System at the beginning of the 1940s.

The South was blessed by adversity in that a depression of lumber prices following 1920 had slowed down the harvesting of the remaining timber and reduced the reckless creation of vast areas of cutover lands until advances had been made in the science of reforestation, especially in the fields of pine genetics and silviculture. In areas where natural seeding was possible an encouraging rate of recovery occurred, and those few conservationists among the lumbermen were given a breathing spell in which to undertake the reclamation of their lands. The Southern Resources Council reported in its two-year study, *The South's Third Forest: A Southern Forest Analysis*:

> By strange paradox, the great depression that began with a crash of the stock market in 1929 lent a helping hand. The general economic decline forced down lumber production in the South to a fraction of its former volume. Subsequently reduction in harvesting requirements gave breathing space for the new forest to grow. Still another factor was reversion of abandoned farms to forest land.
>
> Contrary to earlier predictions, there was no funeral for the southern forest industry in 1930. By the mid-1930's, lumber production began gradually to inch up from the depression-forced depths, then soared again to meet military requirements of World War II on a scale approaching levels of the early 1900's.

Lumbermen, kraft papermakers, and industrial chemists were by no means the only persons involved in the social and economic changes that occurred in the southern forests after 1925. The market for cotton was glutted, the cattle grazing industry was undeveloped, and an almost numberless army of sharecroppers became tenants without land. Millions of acres of southern land had become so badly eroded and leached of nutrients that not even the tenacious hillside sedge grass grew tall enough to cover the undernourished cottontail rabbits. This joint crisis of land and labor was not nearly so disastrous in the long run as contemporary doomsayers proclaimed it to be.

No amount of propagandizing, education, or wise persuasion could have stirred so much movement away from the land, or convinced so many hardheaded and ignorant landowners that they should turn much of their productive energy and land back to the growing of timber as a source of continuing economic improvement. The Great Depression released the necessary amount of unskilled labor to plant trees and otherwise begin the restoration of the land to forest production.

The years of the New Deal opened wide vistas in southern social and economic history. Nothing short of a biting economic depression could have brought into existence the agencies that were to have such a profound impact on the South in such a brief interval of time. By 1936 enough kraft paper mills were in operation to produce 1.3 million tons of paper and cardboard, and for the first time statistics relating to the manufacture of refined white paper began to appear. In the late 1930s the South found itself in a favored position to make rapid advances in the new forest industries.

Some circumstances of southern development that had tended to hold the region back now became assets. Its long history of sparse population and rural isolation left over 100 million acres of potential second-forest lands readily available to supply a continuing stream of raw wood to the rising paper industry. This was an exceedingly fortunate base from which to build an industrial future. The United States Forest Service report *The Forest Situation in the United States* (1932) indicated that the South still had intact 65 percent of its forested area, which could be made immediately productive. Except for some protection from wild fires, however, destructive exploitation of the old timber stand continued. Nationally, said the report, it was clear that to date, "Such restoration of the forest as has occurred, with very rare exceptions, has been a matter of accident rather than usage."

A second government report, *National Pulp and Paper Requirement in Relation to Forest Conservation* (1932), challenged the South to enter the new industrial era of wood utilization. The region, said the report, could manufacture the best grade of newsprint for $27.54 a ton as compared with the prevailing New England and Canadian price of $47.34. Newspapers in the United States in that year spent approximately $200 million for paper and gave promise of increasing that sum substantially in the future.

Not only could the South in time produce a prodigious amount of wood, but it had other valuable advantages in the production of sulphur, limestone, soda, chlorine, alum, rosins, and clays, all necessary additives to the papermaking process. Well before the inroads of the depression were checked, much of the South already sensed that its economic future was brightening. Wrote the editor of the *Blue Book of Southern Progress*, "The South holds possibilities for the expansion of the domestic newsprint industry sufficient to make us independent of foreign sources of supply and several times more than sufficient to satisfy prospective national requirements."

All of this may have seemed within reach of southerners in 1936-1940, but before the promise could be turned into an enduring reality a tremendous effort still had to be made in reshaping southern viewpoints toward renewable forest resources, in redirecting the southern economy, in revising deeply ingrained folk attitudes and ways, in changing the whole pattern of the southern banker mind, and in widening habitually provincial editorial visions. Numerous promotional agencies were to be organized and almost interminable analyses, surveys, and inventories, such as that undertaken by the Southern Forest Experiment Station in New Orleans in 1936, were to be made. Substantial amounts of capital would be required for the building of more paper mills, the organization of a system of continuous wood supply, and the opening of central woodyards. Technically there was still scientific exploration to be carried out in the constant process of refinements; new machines had to be built, and old ones redesigned.

Between the sprouting of a microscopic pine seed on an eroded clump of tired and leached cottonfield soil and its ultimate conversion into a refined product at the terminal end of a papermaking machine were untold miles of human effort, ingenuity, and good luck. For one thing, foresters, farmers, and papermakers had to learn more about pine trees and second-growth hardwoods than was known in 1936. Jubilation over the Herty findings marked only one of many victories that covered a broad front of southern economic and social life in the modern era. Before changes could be brought clearly into realization it was necessary to enlist the energies and resources of governments, industries, institutions, and people. While the southern soils and climate were hospitable to forest growth, prime quality trees did not spring up overnight, nor did a new and largely experimental industry mature instantly in the ancient staple-crop agrarian region.

9. The Grand March South

A forlorn note was sounded in 1923 by R.D. Forbes, who as the first director of the newly authorized Southern Forest Experiment Station had visited large areas of cutover lands. He wrote, "there was quite a ceremony at a southern pine sawmill town the other day, according to the papers. The occasion was the cutting of the last log of the company's timber holdings. When the whistle blew for quitting time, if it was an average Louisiana mill, 77 men were forthwith out of a job. If the output of southern pine drops to eight billion board feet in the next few years, between 80 and 90,000 men must seek employment in other industries."

The last whistle blew in sawmill towns all across the South, a tragic hiatus occurred between the running down of the older lumbering industry and the inception of the new. Although it was evident that forest recovery in the South was speedier than in most other sections of the country, still a substantial amount of time was required by nature to make restitution.

Not only nature, but man had to work magic, through the mastery of scientific timber culture and the development of new manufacturing technology. Nevertheless the forest recovery potential was heartening. None of the commercial tree species was more promising than the slash and loblolly pines, and in Appalachia the hardwoods were capable of healthy restoration. Thus the stage vacated in the mid-1920s by the great saw mills was already reset for the appearance of new and more highly specialized forest industries. Not even Charles H. Herty could have gauged the depth of change that would envelop the South after 1940, even though he had predicted rather extravagantly that the region's pine forest would become a large factor in its salvation.

Repeatedly statisticians had emphasized that if the South continued to butcher its remaining virgin timber stands at the rate it had done in the past the region would conclude its harvest by 1940; so frequently was this warning publicized that it became almost an economic cliche. But, as it happened, by 1930 the demand for southern lumber was substantially reduced. The wooden ship boom had long ago collapsed; automobile manufacturers turned from wood to metal for fabricating wheels and bodies, and the motor car had already doomed the wagon and carriage trade. Manufacturers of farm implements responded to demands for power-driven tools. Thus the traditional prospects of lumber and cotton were simultaneously clouded across a common southern economic horizon.

Lumber production continued to be of major importance, but in a significantly reduced volume; so did the production of crossties, handles, cooperage, mine timbers, telegraph and telephone poles, pilings, and crating. None of these, however, promised a bright or revolutionary future. That belonged to pulpwood and the paper and plywood industries. Reading the signs of the times, Carl Williams of the Federal Farm Board wrote, "It is within the bounds of probability that further substantial development of the pulping industry in the South may take place." Williams based his prediction on the fact that every year since 1920 the region had increased its production of kraft paper pulp.

In considering the rise of the new southern paper industry the historical fact must be kept in mind that by the time of the discoveries made in the chemical laboratory in Savannah the South was already heavily engaged in pulpwood and paper production. In 1930 southern mills produced 600,000 tons of the 883,000 tons of kraft paper manufactured in the United States. The great boom in the industry after 1930 was made possible by refinement and diversification of southern wood products, which made them competitive and profitable. Pioneers in the manufacture of kraft paper who had mills in place to take advantage of the advances in papermaking were those at Hartsville, South Carolina; Roanoke Rapids, North Carolina; Bogalusa, Louisiana; Pensacola, Florida; and Canton, North Carolina. At the latter place the Champion Fibre Company was well established in the production of printing stock from spruce pulpwood, possibly the only refined cellulose fiber paper made in the region. There were veneer mills, but none of them fabricated builder's grade plywood; they turned out mostly laminated packing and boxing materials. No mills produced composition board.

As the South's second forest began to mature, there was a second inrush of diversified wood-using industries to compete with the traditional lumber mills and other wood products manufacturers. In this transitional era the Canadian forester Richard J. Cullen was reported to have observed, "there is going to be the damnedest parade of paper mills here you ever saw." There was, and the newcomers brought to the South distinctly new approaches to exploiting timber resources and to manufacturing wood products. The new industries were both highly diversified and technologically sophisticated. They were not primarily dependent upon the prime lumber quality of standing timber, but concerned themselves with the potential of the renewable resources. To establish a pulp, paper, or plywood mill required large investments for plant, water resources, transportation facilities, and timberlands of many times the acreage of the old single-purpose sawmills. As operative skills and experience increased the new companies were to produce greater volumes of products.

All the necessary elements for the successful operation of pulp, paper, and wood-products mills were present in the South. There were vast areas of cheap abandoned or submarginal croplands, growing national forests, a full reservoir of common labor for harvesting pulpwood and logs, and adequate rail, highway, and water transportation, plus reasonably good port facilities on both the Atlantic and Gulf coasts.

The South into which the post-1930 parade of pulp and paper mills marched was a far different region from that invaded half a century earlier by the sawmill refugees from the northeastern and midwestern cutover areas. Universities and colleges had made marked strides in the organization and maturing of departments of chemistry, physics, biology, and botany, and in the establishment of colleges of business administration. Several of them had organized and staffed departments of forestry. All of the southern states had begun to make discernible headway in combatting the ancient enemies of their forests and in encouraging private landowners to adopt advanced procedures in reforestation and woods management.

Among the newcomers were representatives of the well-established American pulp, paper, and plywood corporations, many of which had rather extensive histories of operations elsewhere. Some were newly organized regional companies whose managements saw promise in the chemical and mechanical advances in the utilization of southern woods.

At the head of the immigrating pack was the Champion Fibre Company, a Cincinnati, Ohio, corporation. This company, like most American corporations, had modest beginnings as a personally owned and operated enterprise. It first manufactured and sold the famous wood-frame schoolroom slates with their traditional red cord trimming. The company's owner, Peter G. Thomson, changed over from the making and sale of slates to printing and publishing specialty books on glazed paper. He was also an inventor who sought to improve the quality of his printed materials, and a pioneer in the development of the halftone process for reproducing photographs by use of almost microscopic dot patterns. To produce sharp images by this new process Thomson needed an evenly coated paper with a uniformly smooth surface. Such paper was not available. He set out to correct this situation by applying his coating materials to the paper stock manufactured by the Champion International Paper Company of Massachussetts, and in 1893 organized the Champion Coated Paper Company.

In the meantime Thomson moved his paper-coating plant from Cincinnati up the Miami River to Hamilton where, despite floods and fires, he succeeded with his growing business. In 1905, searching for a source of wood fiber and paper for his mill, he visited western North Carolina, where scientific forestry was being practiced on the Vanderbilt lands at Biltmore near Asheville. On his first journey Thomson purchased 25,000 acres of spruce lands near Canton in the Blue Ridge. The following year, January 6, 1906, he organized the Champion Fibre Company, and later his son-in-law, Reuben B. Robertson, Sr., drove his family in a wagon from Cincinnati to Canton to take charge of the new company's North Carolina operation. This was to be the beginning of a new era in the history of papermaking in the South.

The Thomson family profited from their new corporation's output. At the beginning of the move southward Peter G. Thomson formed an acquaintance with Biltmore forester Carl Alwin Schenck. Later he gave the Biltmore foresters permission to establish a field station of their school on the Champion Fibre Company's logging site at Sunburst. In the meantime the company employed Walter Damtoft as chief forester. By that time Champion had acquired 100,000 acres of mountain land and was engaged in purchasing more. The new forester was placed in charge of managing the lands owned by Champion and of purchasing additional acreage. Damtoft turned out to be a significant pioneer in southern forest management, applying the latest European methods of management and of keeping records of growth and harvesting. Under his management the Carolina lands made significant returns to the company. Among many accomplishments under Damtoft's supervision was the establishment of ten fire protection districts, which helped to bring the fire menace under some degree of control.

In its formative years of pulpwood production in the mill at Canton, Champion used the calcium bisulphite process to cook the spruce pulp and caustic soda to reduce chestnut and poplar chips. Though the North Carolina spruce resource was a happy find for Champion, the potential supply of this wood was not large and was further reduced in 1930 when the company sold 90,000 acres of its Blue Ridge lands to the federal government to be included in the Great Smoky Mountains National Park. Champion used the $3 million it secured from the Blue Ridge sale to purchase a large tract of pineland in East Texas and to build a new mill.

Once the Herty-Savannah process of cooking yellow pine pulp was introduced, the Champion Fibre Company directed its interest to the piedmont and upper coastal South, and was one of the first companies to profit from the revolution in the utilization of large volumes of southern loblolly and shortleaf pine. In the depression year of 1932 the company embarked upon a much bolder manufacturing venture, and before the end of the decade was producing from both pine and hardwood chips white paper suitable for coating and fine printing stock.

In 1935 the now Hamilton Coated Paper Company was merged with the Champion Fibre Company to become the Champion Paper and Fibre Company. As early as 1917 it had gambled on the future and purchased about 100,000 acres of land in the piedmont, much of it in South Carolina. It also purchased lands in Alabama and Texas. Besides the original paper mill at Canton, the consolidated company in time established pulp and paper mills at Pasadena, Texas, Courtland, Alabama, Roanoke Rapids, North Carolina, and Fort Smith, Arkansas. In 1981 it had mills projected at Halifax, North Carolina, and in Jasper County, Texas. In addition it operated corrugating and packaging mills at various places in the South, where it produced a diversified assortment of commerical products. The big mill at Courtland in northern Alabama had a daily capacity of 800 tons of pulp.

By 1980 the Champion Paper and Fibre Company owned 3.4 mil-

lion acres of American woodlands, about half of which were located
in the South. Standing on Champion's southern lands were a whop-
ping 35 billion board feet of saw timber and over 9 billion cords of
pulpwood. To assure a continuing source of supply for its expanding
plants, this company established three nurseries across the region,
which by 1981 were growing 61 million seedlings a year, a number
almost sufficient to restock the Company's annually harvested and
thinly stocked southern lands. In addition, Champion operated in
1980 three genetically improved seed orchards and five preproduc-
tion seed orchards.

Though Champion was one of the first papermaking immigrants
into the South, it was not to be long without company. After 1935 the
roll of pulp, paper, and fabricated wood products companies grew
long and diversified. It contained such names as International Paper
Company, St. Regis Paper Company, Mead Corporation, Crown-
Zellerbach, Continental Can, Scott Paper Company, Weyerhaeuser,
Westvaco, Masonite, Union-Camp, Bowater Southern Paper Company, Southern Paper Company, Boise-Cascade, United States Plywood, and Georgia-Pacific. There are many others, some of which
are specialized mills, large and small. All, however, by 1960 had staked
out their own forested empires.

Richard J. Cullen's prophecy, made in 1932, that there would be a
thunderous inrush of paper companies to the South was more than
fulfilled by 1984. Cullen himself was to figure prominently in this
movement. He, Erling Riis, and Major J.H. Friend were to play active
roles in the establishment of the International Paper Company south
of the Potomac. After having worked briefly with the Great Southern
Lumber Company mill at Bogalusa, they organized two small companies where they undertook to solve some problems in the manufacture of kraft paper. They then organized in the late 1920s the Bastrop Pulp and Paper Company and the Louisiana Pulp and Paper
Mill. Later these were to be sold to the International Paper Company
to form bases for its entry into the lower South. Along with this trans-
action International procured the management and technical services
of the three ingenious pioneers in the gulf coastal pine pulp industry;
Cullen, Riis, and Friend later became key executives of the International Paper Company.

From Bastrop, International branched out across the South. In
1928 it built a mill at Camden, Arkansas, and the next year one in
Panama City, Florida. A decade later it constructed the big mill in

Georgetown, South Carolina, on the Winyah Bay near the site where the decaying foundations of the old Atlantic Coast Lumber Company were wasting away as shabby memorials to the old industry that had cut out its stand and got out of business without any effort to reclaim its decimated woodlands. There was an interesting historical paradox in the fact that the Georgetown mill was constructed in the heart of the old South Carolina rice belt. International also established mills in the antebellum Mississippi delta cotton belt at Natchez and Vicksburg, Mississippi. At Natchez the company's stacks reared their heads up amongst the ancient plantations and homes, and at Vicksburg under the shadows of the monuments commemorating one of the decisive battles of the Civil War.

There were two fascinating chapters in the history of the International Paper Company's early years in the South. In the woodlands the company had purchased from the Atlantic Coast Lumber Company, its foresters located on Kilsock Bay a superior longleaf pine sapling, which had stuck its head above ground in 1935; within twenty years it had attained a height of seventy-two feet and a girth diameter at breast height of fifteen inches. This was proclaimed "the most superior tree in all the forests of the South." Foresters labeled it in bold white paint "no. 1." They shot buds from its high branches with rifles, drilled holes in its trunk with increment augers to lay bare its innermost secrets of growth and physical well-being, and in October they gathered its ripening burrs from which to extract their precious seeds. The buds were grafted onto commoner root stock to perpetuate the Kilsock aristocracy in greater numbers.

In 1940 International had planted 179 million trees by the old hand-and-foot-dibble method. This, however, became too laborious and costly a method of reforestation to serve expanding future needs. Ed Porter, manager of the company's southern woodlands, was intrigued by the mechanical planters that neighboring Georgia tobacco farmers used to plant their spring crops. Under his supervision a Valdosta machinist created a tree planter that could be drawn by a tractor over rough fields and would give its operators a signal on an eight-foot spacing.

While International was expanding other companies were doing likewise. One of these was Westvaco (originally West Virginia Paper Company), which did not penetrate as deeply into the South as did several of its competitors, but whose mills in Virginia, Maryland, and South Carolina have large daily capacities. This has been especially true of the mill at Charleston, which in 1977 consumed just slightly under 2,000 cords of pulpwood daily. Like some of the earlier companies Westvaco was able to acquire a large land base between the Atlantic Coast and Columbia, South Carolina. It took advantage of the availability of large blocks of sandhill lands at bargain prices.

Subsequent immigrants to the southern woodlands such as St. Regis, Weyerhaeuser, Bowaters, and Boise Cascade also had to acquire sufficient landholds to ensure ample supplies of raw materials for their large mills. The Weyerhaeuser Corporation entered the lower South because of the rapid renewal capacity of the native loblolly pine. When measured against the growth of forests in the Northwest, the southern pine cycle increased wood production by three- or fourfold. This giant corporation from the far Northwest purchased its first landholds in Mississippi and Alabama in 1954. The following year it purchased 45,000 acres from the Murphy Corporation in a land exchange arrangement, and in 1966-67 the company acquired approximately 100,000 acres from the Flintkote Company in Kemper County, Mississippi. At the same time it purchased the holdings of the Deweese Lumber Company in adjoining Neshoba County. By 1980 Weyerhaeuser had accumulated holdings of 700,000 acres and had established wood-using plants at Bruce, Philadelphia, and Columbus, Mississippi, and at Lamar, Alabama.

The implications of Weyerhaeuser's migration to the South were all but staggering. Never before had Mississippians had to comprehend so vast an enterprise. In November 1981 an investigative reporter from the Jackson *Clarion-Ledger* stirred a momentary tempest in the state's political teapot over the location and construction of four mill units at Columbus. His articles implied that the incumbent governor, during his campaign for office, had made promises about the location of the Weyerhaeuser mill. It was hinted that the Mississippi Agricultural and Industrial Board, along with some local officials, were unduly influenced by the company. The reporter also said that the Northeast Mississippi Building and Construction Trade Council objected to negotiating private instead of public construction contracts; it was said that the Council feared exclusion of union labor from this vast construction job.

There were prompt denials of any irregular actions by public officials, and apparently the storm was allayed almost as suddenly as it had blown up. The reporter possibly overstated his information. An interesting and no doubt substantial fact revealed in this public flurry was that Mississippi traded Weyerhaeuser an extended lease on a sixteenth section of publicly reserved school lands for 666 acres of company-owned pinelands. The state could only grant a lease, not a clear title, to this land under terms of the Southwest Ordinance reserve of 1790, and had to purchase the lease of local private lessors.

When the initial unit of the Columbus complex, near the Tombigbee River sixteen miles from Columbus, was announced Weyerhaeuser and state and local officials said the new mill would cost $750 million and would generate an annual payroll of approximately $27 million; the cotton crop of 1981 in seven southern states yielded $678 million. The Columbus plant, located on a 9,000-acre site, was the most costly one built in the corporation's eighty-two-year history.

Running at full capacity the Columbus mill is capable of producing 500 tons of lightweight coated paper a day. Its furnaces consume shredded bark and other waste material stripped from long-log pine stock to generate enough electricity to supply 11,500 homes. This current is sold to the Tennessee Valley Authority on a special "sell-buy-back" agreement. Not far away in Greene County, Alabama, the company operates a forest regenerating center (nursery) capable of producing hundreds of millions of seedlings to replant clear-cut lands.

Viewed against the southern agrarian background, the economic and sociological implications of a modern forest-industries plant like that at Columbus establish a dramatic gauge of the depth of change occurring in the modern South. When this particular mill was being readied for operation the company received 10,000 applications to fill 380 jobs. By the time the first roll of coated paper was ready to be loaded in a freight car Weyerhaeuser had invested approximately a million dollars per job in the construction of the power plant and a single paper unit. In addition it had organized an educational program to train employees to operate the highly sophisticated and electronically automated plant.

Beyond the boundaries of Columbus and Lowndes County, the Weyerhaeuser tentacles reach deep not only into Mississippi and Alabama, but into the entire South. The growth of genetically improved loblolly pines on 700,000 acres of company-owned lands not only involves scientific and management talents, but likewise reshapes the conditions of life for a good portion of the regional population. Thousands of people are affected by the presence of the mill: pulpwood cutters and haulers, landowners, merchants, equipment dealers, repairmen, and the professional services.

But what of the 9,620 people whose applications for jobs at Weyerhaeuser's Columbus operation were rejected? Can the new southern industries ever employ large numbers of unskilled native labor? Where will they all fit into the future economic and social systems? Even in the woods themselves, where the most unskilled of laborers in the wood-products industries have been employed, modern timbering equipment has relieved men of the laborious tasks of sawing and loading pulpwood and "long" logs, and the replanting of the clear-cut lands has now become largely a mechanical procedure. Across the butts of the great piles of long logs in woodyards and at the mills are the tell-tale scorings of the mechanical harvester, which has consigned the chainsaw to the more menial jobs of limbing and topping.

Located in the very path of frontier advancement into the old cotton lands on its large tract of the Mississippi black belt, the Weyerhaeuser complex symbolizes dramatically the rise of an entire different social and economic age from the region's immediate past. A historian dealing with the rise of the most modern of the Souths has difficulty reconciling modern industries with the South depicted in the literature of the depression era. Nor can he see in the new southern worker—the worker able to secure employment in these plants—the image of the unskilled peons of the past.

Over and over the histories of the marchers in the great wood-users' parade into the South can be traced back to relatively small individually owned and operated companies. Within a century they became highly diversified corporations. None epitomized the great American success story more than Colonel Daniel Mead's tiny paper company of Dayton, Ohio, which had its beginnings in 1846.

In 1981 the Mead Company owned 680,000 acres of prime southern pinelands in South Carolina, Georgia, and Alabama, and drew timber stock from 1.6 million acres through its joint ownership with the Brunswick Pulp and Paper Company and the Georgia Pulp and Paper Company. In addition it had access to a sufficient supply of Appalachian hardwood stock in Tennessee, Kentucky, and Alabama to support its plant in Kingsport, Tennessee, and its large corrugated paperboard mill at Stevenson, Alabama.

Mead is one of the more highly diversified companies in the South. It manufactures fine printing and writing papers, corrugated board stock, cellophane shrink packaging, plywood, and lumber. Much of the bleached pulp produced in the Brunswick mill is shipped away to be converted into refined papers at Kingsport, Chillicothe, Ohio, and Menasha, Wisconsin. In addition to the production of pulp, the Georgia companies operate saw and plywood mills with the capacity to produce 110 million board feet of lumber and 110 million square feet of plywood annually.

Like Peter G. Thomson's Champion Fibre Company, Mead made an early entry into the mountain South when it purchased a tanning extract mill at Kingsport and converted it into a pulp mill. In the grand invasion after 1930 it purchased joint interest in the Georgia mills, and in 1975 brought into operation the large paperboard mill at Stevenson, Alabama. The Georgia and Alabama mills had the capacity to produce 1.5 million tons of paper and board annually. In the case of the Kingsport and Stevenson mills it was unnecessary for Mead to purchase lands because private and public landowners were able to assure them a stable supply of wood. In 1981, Mead may have been the only major paper company in the South wholly dependent upon noncorporation lands to supply its wood resources.

Reminiscent of the early immigration of the northern textile mills to the South in the last quarter of the nineteenth century, the move of St. Regis Paper Company of New England was characteristic of the invasion of the southern forested region by an outside company. The history of the St. Regis Company dates back to 1808 when Gurdon Caswell, an industrious Connecticut Yankee, began the manufacture of rag paper in Watertown, New York. This tiny hand-operated enterprise, disrupted frequently by drunken sprees, became the foundation ultimately for a major southern forest-based industry. During its first half-century of existence the company increased its sales and made technological improvements and refinements, many of them the results of yankee mechanical ingenuity. Like the Champion Fibre Company, St. Regis in 1824 published books. It produced editions of such famous titles as Webster's *spelling book* and Pope's *Essay on Man*. The Civil War and its accelerated demands for paper gave the business in Watertown a phenomenal boost.

During the post–Civil War decades the St. Regis Company began using more and more cellulose fiber to supplement the rag content of its product. In 1899 the company was incorporated and began a period of expansion under the leadership of C.H. Remington. In the early twentieth century the St. Regis organization experienced other mergers and with them changes in personnel. By 1940 it had become firmly established in the manufacturing of bags and packaging. One of its products was ideally suited to the sanitary bagging of granu-

lated sugar, flour, meal, and other bulk staples. As American merchandising underwent revolutionary changes in the packaging of all
sorts of goods, St. Regis expanded its manufacturing facilities to serve
the new demands.

As the heavy bag industry grew there was an increasing demand
for stouter kraft paper. St. Regis turned to the rising papermaking
resources of the southern forest lands. In 1946 it purchased James H.
Allen's Florida Pulp and Paper Company at Pensacola, Florida. Allen,
a self-taught forester, and the famous paper scientist R.J. Cullen had
established, with loans from the Reconstruction Finance Corporation, small mills in Louisiana, Arkansas, Mississippi, Alabama, and
Georgia. Following the St. Regis purchase, Allen became vice chairman of St. Regis and a member of its board of directors.

By 1977 St. Regis had established mills at Monticello, Mississippi,
and Pensacola, Florida, with an annual consumption capacity of nearly
4 million cords of pulpwood. In 1891 the corporation owned 2.4 million acres of timberlands in Florida, Alabama, Mississippi, Louisiana,
and Texas. It maintained pine nurseries at Lee, Florida, and Jasper,
Texas, which produced genetically superior seedlings. Officials of the
company indicate that it follows a rotation of twenty to thirty-two
years as compared with a maturity span of sixty to ninety years in its
northeastern forests and of sixty to a hundred years in the Northwest. St. Regis's southern woods are controlled by aid of computers,
which are connected with the eighteen-day scanning cycle of the National Aeronautics and Space Administration's Landsat II satelite. By
this means the company can detect any changes in its vast forest
holdings.

Maps appearing in *Southern Pulpwood Production*, 1977, and in
Lockwood's *Directory of Pulp and Paper Mills in the United States*, 1979,
give a graphic sense of the expansion of these industries across the
South. For the latter year there were 115 mills already in operation,
which consumed 110,000 tons of wood a day. Annually the region as
a whole produced a staggering 54 million standard cords of wood and
plant by-products, with Alabama, Georgia, and Mississippi being the
leading producing states. It is almost impossible to arrive at a true
total cash return from this material because of the variable prices paid
for stumpage and by-products. Cordwood sales alone for the three
leading producing states in 1974 were over $645 million. By that year
the South was producing approximately two-thirds of the nation's
paper stock. A conservative stumpage estimate for pine cordwood in

the South as a whole in 1977, at $9.00 a cord, would have been over $4 billion to timberland owners alone. The return in wages and material prices at least tripled this amount, and by conversion into pulp, paper, plywood, and pebbleboard the ultimate value was increased manyfold.

It must be emphasized that because of the nature of the public corporate structure and the biregional operations of the manufacturers it is difficult to arrive at even a reasonable guess as to how much of the capital gain from the industry remains in the South. The modern wood-using industries represent a wide diversity of ownership, including many investors who could not with certainty distinguish between a loblolly pine tree and a metropolitan fire hydrant. Though the management personnel can be identified, and local representatives personify the companies, the actual ownership is as remote and diversified as the international marketing and investment complex. These corporations, of course, are not alone in their wide diversity of ownership and control. They do, however, represent about as completely extraregional ownership and top management as any industry in the South. Most of the corporate offices are located in New York, Tacoma, Dayton, Stamford, and England. There is one interesting exception: Georgia-Pacific has transferred its corporate offices from the West Coast to Atlanta.

Despite the reams of published figures, therefore, a full picture of the financial implications of the new wood-using industries is difficult to bring into focus. The Mississippi Agricultural and Forestry Experiment Station in 1978 published an analysis, based upon data for 1974-75, of the economic contributions of forestry to that state. There were said to be approximately 17 million forested acres in the state's 30.3 million acres of landed area; and forests yielded $327 million in wages in 1975. In that year the volume of pulpwood harvested achieved a near balance with that of saw timber delivered to the mills. In addition to general income from harvested stock, the state was said to have collected nearly $14 million in ad valorem taxes. The analysts emphasized that only 60 percent of the Mississippi timberland potential had been realized. If the full growing capacity had been realized at 1975 prices, the added capital return would have been $164 million and there would have been an increase of 5,060 jobs. If, in addition to full productivity of available timberlands, intensive management had been practiced, it was estimated that the increased return would have been $584 million with an addition of 23,630 new jobs.

What was true in Mississippi no doubt was equally true in at least six of the other major southern pulpwood producing states, with only one difference: some of the others had much higher comparative industrial incomes from other sources. At any rate it can be assumed that the combined income from all wood-using industries easily outstripped that from the growing of staple crops and cattle grazing.

Whereas the old timber industries had a profound but fleeting social and economic impact on their communities, the new industries will have more lasting results. Because the establishment of sophisticated wood-fiber plants is such a costly undertaking a community can be reasonably assured that a plant has come to stay. In earlier days even major sawmill operations did not have such a wide-ranging impact as do modern pulp, paper, and plywood installations, which have immediate access to the diversity of transportation facilities that enable them to reach over long distances for supplies of raw materials and to seek widely dispersed world markets for their finished products. Just as important is the capability of the new industries to manufacture innovative products to serve a highly diversified consumer public.

And to the modern corporations the land is the base of continuous reconversion. There will never again be such a thing as a great desert of cutover lands. Areas now denuded of timber stand become a prime field for replanting to assure a future crop. This means that corporate acquisitions of lands have a pronounced aspect of finality. So far as can be known, lands transferred to corporate ownership are locked in perpetuity; there will be no further history in the heavily timbered areas of estate dissolutions or public land sales.

The private noncommercial timberland owner continues to produce the greater volume of wood, but despite the advice of federal, state, and corporate foresters the private landowners too often allow their woods to produce only 40 to 60 percent of their potential. Though little is said specifically in corporate reports about self-sufficiency, corporate land departments are vigilant to buy every acre of land possible. The arrival of each new corporation in the South intensifies the campaign to purchase land bases.

In many areas of the South, very little land is now available to yeoman farmers. And in a period of inflated interest rates, increased fuel and implement costs, and softening of prices for agricultural products, many farmers, even those engaged in agribusiness, have been priced off the land. With each decennial census more rural southerners have shifted over into the class of rural nonfarm or city-dwelling wage earners. Much of the traditional ruralness that once gave tone to regional life and provincial flavor to politics, religion, and literature has disappeared from the South.

The modern southern wood-using industries with their scientifically trained personnel have created new classes of employment in southern economic society. Unskilled laborers such as pulpwood cutters, woodyard rustlers, and tree planters form new social islands within old agrarian communities. In 1972 it was estimated that 3.6 million employees were associated with the timber industry in the South. But the new mills have not given rise to industrial villages with isolated social and economic castes, like those seen in earlier days in the textile, turpentine, and lumber industries. The army of timber industry employees in 1972 included 48,700 in the field of management and 97,500 employed directly in the harvesting of timber. The rest were engaged in forest management, manufacturing, and shipping. It is difficult, however, in human terms to bring into detailed focus the entire chain of production from the planting of trees through season after season of growth to final harvest by sweaty sun-scorched laborers, struggling in annoying ground cover and over rough terrain, up through the handling of wood in gathering yards and on into the mills and the production of sophisticated newsprint, book and magazine printing papers, the wrappings of tomorrow's bread, or the fluffy swadling clothes of a rising new generation of infants.

There are dynamic forces in changing American and world economies that will affect the future of the forest industries. Among these are increasing population, changing social tastes and merchandising practices, and changing styles of home life. Overlooked or not clearly described in much of the voluminous statistical and descriptive materials is the impact of American advertising, public health crusades, and the national antiseptic taste upon the southern forest industry. The packaging of every sort of merchandise from nails, groceries, and cosmetics to books and underwear has become a major industry in itself. Yearly additional commodities and goods once displayed and sold in an unpackaged state are enclosed in transparent envelopes.

Weyerhaeuser, in its 1980 annual report, gave some emphasis to the development of its "soft disposables" business. The company expressed pride in its disposable diapers, which three of its plants produced and which were sold under private labels. The social and economic impact of this phase of the cellulose business alone has tremendous implications for modern American society, which constantly seeks means to escape the rigors of life in an earlier age.

Charles Herty and his colleagues in the tiny Savannah laboratory in 1931 only initiated the new scientific age in the use of southern wood cellulose fibers. Scarcely a year has gone by that the industry's scientists, along with those in public institutional laboratories, have not introduced better techniques for handling old problems, or introduced new wood-based products. Outside the laboratory applied land and forest management experience and knowledge have insured a type of continuity in southern economic growth and stability that was largely lacking in the earlier lumber business.

By no means, however, has the southern lumber business gone into eclipse. In all the excitement over the coming of the new corporations after 1930 this industry has attracted less public attention than it did when it occupied the center stage in earlier years. Nevertheless it is of wide diversity and is still of major significance. The industry embraces the harvesting of large volumes of timber for lumber, poles, fence posts, crossties, pallets, veneer, plywood, pilings, bridge timbers, and many other special uses. Whatever competition it may face from the composition and prefabricated building materials, lumber is still the basic domestic building material. The South has almost a monopoly on the major hardwood market and it supplies an appreciable portion of the softwoods. In its report *Forest Statistics of the U.S.*, 1977, the United States Forest Service designated four southern timber-producing regions, which contained 107 million acres of forested lands. These regions produced over 26.6 billion board feet of lumber as compared with an estimated 100 billion feet nationally. The entire eastern part of the United States produced 35.3 billion board feet, while all other regions, including Alaska, produced 66.2 billion board feet. Many of the pulp and paper companies also operate lumber and plywood mills in which they convert better grades of timber into building stock, make two-by-fours out of their plywood cores, and make pebble or composition board out of the sawdust and other residue. Even sawdust and pine bark have become saleable commodities.

Nearly all the wood-using companies that came south after 1932 received some kind of direct encouragement from the various states in which they located their mills. State development boards, legislators, governors, and chambers of commerce all were alert to the long-run economic implications of the newer types of timber industries. Legislators in South Carolina held out inducements to Bowaters by revising an old populist law that limited the amount of land a foreign corporation could acquire within the state. All the states built special access roads and improved others, and river and port authorities became acutely aware of the need for adequate docking and shipping facilities.

In the first burst of the modern South's drive to entice new institutions into its borders, the wood-using industries were welcomed with open arms. Few negative questions were asked, environmentalists made few if any protests, and communities asked only that the companies bring with them fat payrolls. Only after the publication of Rachel Carson's *Silent Spring* (1962), and the rise in national importance of the Sierra Club, the Audubon Society, and other environmental groups, were local sensitivities to the location and operation of the mills stirred, as indicated in the protest over possible air and water pollution by the Union-Camp paper mill to be located at Eastport, South Carolina, in 1981. The earlier and more offensive paper mills experienced only minimal objections—at least prior to their construction—over environmental pollution. After the mills were in operation and began emitting obnoxious atmospheric fumes there were local complaints, but as one wiseacre observed, the local communities were generally willing to tolerate environmental pollution because the smell of a paper mill was also the sweet smell of jobs and cash incomes. Perhaps no mill anywhere in the South created greater atmospheric contamination than the pioneer Champion mill at Canton, North Carolina. This mill was located in a geographical situation highly conducive to industrial fogging. On damp and overcast days the fumes are trapped in the Pigeon River Valley between steep ridges and create a rather heavy atmospheric condition. The technically advanced Weyerhaeuser mill at Columbus, Mississippi, on the other hand, emits no discernible odor. Possibly as a result of public pressure, recent annual reports of large paper companies record heavy expenditures for pollution control.

Environmental concern has also focused on the conservation and propagation of wildlife in the new forests. In this area, the corporations, foresters, and even private landholders have made a favorable showing. While it is true to a considerable extent that pinewoods are not the most favorable feeding grounds for most game, heavy grass and weed cover during the early years of reforestation of clear-cut fields provide good forage. In many, if not most cases, the pinewood sterility is interrupted by creek and river bottoms, and brushlined hollows and ravines. In Appalachia, in large areas of both corporate and public forests, much of the original wildlife population is beginning to be restored. That is also true in the piedmont woodlands, where deer and wild turkeys have returned in large numbers despite the eternal vandalism of human poachers. Although the clear-cutting and replanting of large areas of woods in the early stages of regrowth present a desolate scene to many conservationists, the resulting cover has proved conducive to increasing the game population.

Under prevailing modern practices it is not likely that there will ever again be established in the South any appreciable area of virgin forest comparable to the first forest. The corporations' computer system will prevent this. Every company's forest management is attuned to a rotation system having a fixed span of approximately twenty years, and the computer is a persistent nudger reminding field crews that the harvesting and reforestation cycles are at hand.

But the modern wood-using corporations have given material assistance to southern forest agencies in the creation of an awareness of the heavy financial losses caused by forest fires, disease, and insect damage, and have demonstrated the profitability of reclaiming marginal lands by reforestation. Never before in the history of the South has such a large proportion of the population been made so acutely sensitive to the long-range significance of the region's timber resource.

The march of the mills into the South has been incessant since 1930. New ones are brought "on line" almost every year. With the introduction of new products, changes in American life styles, and the increase of older standard products, the South gains a larger stake in the national economy on the one hand and undergoes more revolutionary social and economic changes on the other. No longer are the humble pine tree and the towering tulip poplar and oak trees of the broader stretches of historic woods and wornout cotton fields an unobtrusive bounty of nature. They represent a means of ultimately tying the South to an unfolding age of science with the bonds of soil, climate, geography, and chemistry, bonds King Cotton could never fully forge. The great parade of wood-using mills since the Savannah laboratory successes has ushered into being a New South neither Henry W. Grady, Captain Francis W. Dawson, nor any other contemporary soothsayer of a new age could have comprehended.

10. Rearranging the Land

Daily in the modern South an economic and social conflict continues that has greater impact than any armed conflict that ever occurred in the land. This quiet but powerful force is steadily revising much of the foundation of southern culture and human relationships with the land. The daily struggle is not between political, racial, or social groups, but between competitors who contend for access to the land for forest and nonforest uses. If large landholds in parts of the antebellum South represented wealth, power, and social leadership, big landholding in the present South represents a tremendous base of both private and corporate wealth.

The Pine Forest Task Force estimated in 1959 that every dollar paid at the stump for pulpwood contributed $16 to the regional economy, and every million acres producing $10 worth of pulpwood per acre added $480 million. Since that date, of course, inflation has enormously increased the magnitude of the figures, but the relationship remains valid. Thus the recorded loss in the decade 1969-1979 of 7.4 million acres of forest in the fourteen southern states has vital implications for the South.

It may be that it is no longer historically accurate to speak of the current woods of the South as either the "second" or "third forest." The process of timber production is a continuous one of clear-cutting, scraping the land bare, and replenishing it with superior pine and hardwood stock. On major timber holdings of both private and corporate owners there are established rotations, many of these determined by computerized programs. There is no longer a major climax of tree growth.

Segments of the new southern forest are to be seen everywhere. They line interstate and local highways, creep silently up to town and city limits, crowd up to modern airport runways, and their darkening enclosures even fold about country churches and family cemeteries. The ever-broadening belt of submarginal land converted to its original state of growing trees has already had enormous effects upon the lives of millions of southerners in terms of personal income, creation of new tax bases, development and support of institutions, and a broad spectrum of environmental conditions. This transformation of land-use pattern has even had a major bearing on racial and political affairs in the South.

Every year since 1930 has seen larger portions of the old agricultural cropland of the South come under the management of private and corporate owners who have converted them solely to the growing of timber. Annually more and more areas of the region are being stripped down to bare earth, again laying open to view the ravages of cotton and other staple-crop culture. Temporarily at least the land is once again left open to losses from erosion. Luckily the bulldozed and disced earth is now planted to fast-growing superpines and hardwood stock, which hastens the matting of the land with needle and leaf mold and shortens the generation span as compared with trees sprung from natural seeding.

Modern forestry management is aimed largely at obliterating the marks of past abuses of the land. Like alien outer-space monsters, oversized bulldozers crash through undergrowth, weed trees, stumps, honeysuckle vines, over gullies, and even over abandoned tenant cabins with the irresistible force of an avenging angel. Their slashing blades put a thousand medieval swordsmen to shame. These behemoths crawl over the land in clanking strides, turning up as much soil in a day's time as twenty old-fashioned plowboys could break in a cotton-growing season. In a half-dozen passes a bulldozer can smash into oblivion familiar and revered landmarks, objects cherished by generations of southerners. Time-and-weather-stained southern mansions about whose hearths were woven the tapestry of so much of human history, and from beneath whose rooftrees came politicians, professional men and women, and staunch citizens are splintered and ground into debris in hours. Double parlors, powder rooms, and sweeping hallways with stair landings where in flush days of cotton culture southern belles robed and preened themselves in style, were courted and married, and where their children were conceived and born are smashed into mounds of debris.

In another age these houses were family monuments. In mansion and cabin alike men and women died and their corpses lay in sorrowful wakes in their final hours above ground. On their porches harried farmers once sat and stared into leaden skies hoping for crop-saving rains, or there they pondered the creeping paralysis of ever-mounting debts and the certainty of crop failures and mortgage foreclosures. Joyful or morose, these vanishing houses were not only monuments of southern family history, but likewise of a whole regional way of life. From their doors volunteers hurried away to join Confederate regiments in the Civil War, and four years later returned to make fresh beginnings. From them callow youths went away to college or went out into the world bare-knuckled and, either way, came home changed.

All the old sentimentalities, the substance of folk memories grown brighter and more heartening in the conversations of old men and women, centered in the old houses and about the ancient landmarks. Within heartless minutes monsters bearing the names John Deere, Caterpillar, or Case, not Sherman or Grant, pound a century or more of southern civilization and human physical history into smears of pulverized rubble. Only battered and scarred chimney rocks are left scattered about to mark family seats. Along with the houses have gone smokehouses, barns, garden spots, and beloved old foot-paths—all crushed to a common plane of earthly oblivion. Only memories and the scattered shards of china and glassware, shattered artifacts of another time and another condition of life, remain behind as evidence of earlier human occupancy.

On the broader pattern of the land itself familiar old landmark trees are knocked down to perish in piles of brush put under the torch. Boundaries of old fields, so familiar to plowmen and cotton-choppers, have been erased; even old farms themselves are merged until the mosaic of property boundaries registered in the county clerk's office no longer has meaning. One can stand and look out over vast fields laid bare by modern machines and bring up visions of men and mules gouging away at the soil with their primitive plows and hoes. Across these new weed-strewn vistas, in which regularly spaced rows of genetically improved pines push up their heads, the facing vistas of the South's past merge into those of its intensified industrial future. Occasionally stone-age artifacts turn up, made and dropped down by an ancient brown race who left little other evidence of their having lived and wandered beneath the South's first forest. Intermixed with these intriguing remains are those of a later and now dispersed civilization: here a mule shoe, a pants button, a rust-encrusted heel bolt, or an old-fashioned iron cottonbale tie. The great discs dredge up eroded plowshares, once bought "on the credit" from a furnishing merchant on usurious terms.

Over the land now springing up in orderly planned and planted forest rows, the melodious eventide yodeling of cotton hands heralding the end of day is no longer heard. In their place is the angry whine of the chain saw and the furious roar of timberjacks, bulldozers, and pulpwood trucks grinding their way across gullies, over ancient washed furrows, over terraces, creeping forward with unbelievably heavy burdens of pulpwood and logs.

One of the most forlorn monuments to the past is the southern country church, which once sheltered a large membership but now stands virtually shadeless and deserted amidst a thousand-acre corporate-owned timber tract, its windows staring vacantly out upon the void of the land, giving the appearance of an aged senile man whose mind is stuck in the past. Quickly the church and its adjoining graveyard will become sealed within a vacuum created by commercial forests that crowd members off the land and scatter congregations.

In many other ways the face of the South is changed. Where once roads were crowded with cotton and crosstie wagons there are now pulpwood, long-log trucks, and bin trucks hauling sawdust and shavings. Pulpwood trucks with their characteristic three steel stanchions, clanging stickloader cables, and battered bodies long ago replaced farm wagons and mules. The woodyard has crowded the cotton gin off the face of the region, and Friday afternoon paydays have neutralized the importance of southern village and small-town Saturdays. Now even the day of the ugly pulpwood trucks is numbered by the appearance of the air-conditioned, heavy-duty long-log vehicles, which haul astonishingly heavy loads of full-length trees. With every passing year bringing less and less demand for arduous and sweaty human labor, it may well happen soon that mechanical shears and gasoline- and diesel-powered skidders and loaders will banish the pulpwood truck and its three- and five-man crews of share-workers.

A combination of events has accounted for dispossession of large segments of the southern population from the land. With the increased mechanization of agriculture, tenant farmers gave way to the new machines, non-row crops, and the restored forests. An appreciable portion of the rural southern population, and blacks in particular, moved into string towns along highways or went to towns and cities away from the lands on which they and their fathers before them had labored in tobacco and corn fields. Those laborers who transferred from field to forest became pulpwood cutters and haulers. Many a southern pulpwood producer cuts trees from old fields where once his parents drudged away their lives as tenant farmers. Though present-day homes in the new rural nonfarm string towns and villages are far superior to those of the old sawmill towns and turpentine camps, many of them still bear the blighting marks of social isolation.

During the past half-century since Charles H. Herty and his fellow chemists and paper engineers at Savannah helped clear the last major hurdle to the production from southern woods of newsprint and more refined paper products, changes have occurred in the South that may have had a greater bearing upon the region's long-run history than most of those that occurred before 1930. None has been more revolutionary than the fact that potentially productive timberlands, which once exchanged owners for little more financial consideration than the payment of delinquent taxes, have now increased phenomenally in both value and long-range use.

Columns in newspapers and farm journals in timber producing sections reflect the depth of the revolution brought about by the new wood-using industries. No longer are there baffling technological barriers to future utilization of both pine and hardwoods in the manufacture of a galaxy of industrial products. Chemists constantly introduce new processes and refinements in the conversion of cellulose fibers into commercial products. There are promising indications that future generations of Americans may even look to the abundant growth of southern "trash" or "weed" trees as a source for the distillation of methanol and other wood chemical fuels.

While chemists experiment with further utilization of cellulose bases, mechanics have been diligent in the perfection of chipping, slicing, pressing, and gluing machines, which long ago made archaic the old-fashioned southern sawmill surrounded by its great stacks of rough-sawn lumber and its smoking shaving towers, sawdust piles, and slab pits.

The pulpwood dealer and his woodyard have replaced the cotton buyer with his huge sheet-metal warehouse and car-siding platforms. There still is a furnishing trade, but instead of credit-granting merchants it is conducted by pulpwood buyers and by truck and chainsaw dealers, sometimes by the new plywood companies. It is not at all unusual for a truck to be worn out by the time it is paid for, and producers, like the old-line cotton tenants, never really find themselves free of debt. New models and new machines appear on the market, each more expensive than the one it replaces, necessitating a far more fluid flow of credit than cotton farmers could ever have conceived.

Meanwhile in laboratories, nurseries, and orchards geneticists have introduced at least three generations of selectively bred growth stock. Continuous research in this area brightens the promise of the South's primary position in the production of a growing list of finished wood-based materials. Almost every nursery season introduces advances in the quality of seedling stock.

Never before in the history of the South have landowners been so receptive of scientific information as to land management, silviculture, fire prevention, insect and disease control, and the modernization of harvesting techniques. No prophet in 1920 would have been so rash as to predict that southern farmers would accept a tax levy for the purpose of preventing and combatting forest fires. It would be a rare exception if a traveller through the South today heard a farmer complaining of this tax. At no time in the past has care of the land and forest been so important to the private timberland owner.

Though many of the corporations maintain active vigilance for possible land purchases, it is still the private southern tree farmer who owns most of the land and produces the greater bulk of wood for industrial use. Next in ownership of southern land is the Federal Government. In 1977 it owned 23.5 million acres of productive southern commercial timberlands. County and state governments owned an additional 8 million acres. In all, private corporate owners accounted for 133 million acres. Under prevailing economic and political conditions, and with highly inflated southern land prices, it is unlikely that any appreciable additions can be made to the national forests. There even might appear to be an ultimate limit on the acreage the wood-using corporations can obtain, this despite the fact that some of the old-line northwestern companies have migrated southward and still manage, at high cost, to put together enough landhold to sustain their mills.

The more pressing question, however, is how much of the present timbered area in the South can be retained in production. Forested areas are yearly being reduced by expanding urban communities, insatiable shopping malls, development of industrial plants, nuclear utility generating stations, thousands of miles of powerlines and pipelines, interstate highways, and other uses incompatible with timber production. The very natural elements, so conducive to tree growing, also threaten the region with competition for land, for the shift of industry and population to the sunbelt involves land withdrawal. Present projections are that the South will lose 200,000 acres of forest lands annually between 1982 and 2000, and this perhaps is a too-conservative prediction.

The bedrock fact that faces southern forest conservation and production is the ancient folk adage, "They ain't making no more land." Thus the major thrust in the future is not so much toward land acquisition and conversion, but to a vastly more efficient system of management and utilization of that already under wooded cover. This means that better quality trees must replace present inferior stands in order to increase the rate of maturity. The shortages predicted in view of what the prophets say will be the demand for all kinds of cellulose products in the twenty-first century may well be a blessing. Now growing on approximately 100 million acres of southern lands is a stand of inferior trees that shade out and destroy those of usable commercial quality. If the present talk of supplementing fossil fuels with methanol ever materializes into widespread demand this stand of trashy growth would not be a waste after all.

Whatever may have been southern laggardness in areas of comparative statistics with other regions of the nation, and with world areas for that matter, the South now enjoys an assured prime position in forest production. Other areas of the United States, South America, Canada, Western Europe, the Soviet Union, and parts of the Orient can, in scope of time, produce competitive amounts of wood, but none, not even the rich timberlands of Canada, Scandinavia, and the Soviet Union, approach the recovery growth in the South. The region can make from two to five rotations to one in the colder and less favored soils in other parts of the world. From the outset of English settlement on the southern Atlantic Coast there has been an increasing export demand for southern lumber and forest products, but nothing like the proportions of the present. Annually the export of lumber, logs, plywood, masonite, pebbleboard, and paper has increased.

Running throughout the federal and state forestry publications, those of wood-using corporations, and in the public press there is an awareness that the South is in a favored economic position in this area. In an address to employees and stockholders of the St. Regis

Paper Company, which appeared in that corporation's publication *Reach*, William R. Haselton, chairman and chief executive officer, wrote in August, 1981:

> The question is, can America supply the necessary raw materials to meet the domestic needs while sustaining increased exports in the years to come? The answer is definitely "yes"
>
> A portion of this additional timber will come from increased harvest on national forests. The major amount, however, will originate from that large and productive section of country lying south of the Mason-Dixon Line, between the Atlantic Ocean and the plains of Texas. This area is warm, fertile, accessible, easy to plant and manage and capable in the next 20 to 30 years of doubling its annual output of trees. Beginning in this decade, we should witness a new ascendancy in the South as that area assumes the role in the world timber market comparable to the place the region once held in the 18th and 19th centuries in the cotton and tobacco industries.

If there still remains a substantial barrier in the field of southern wood uses, it is in the full consumption of all wood fiber grown in trash trees in the region. The volume of cellulose is present on most of the timberland, but the processing of all of it for practical and profitable use remains a challenge. For instance, if the scrub trees and cluttering understory on national forest lands alone were fully utilized there would be enough raw materials to sustain several appreciable industries for years to come. The Daniel Boone National Forest in Kentucky would alone supply a major fiber-producing industry in continuous operation from now to eternity by just removing smothering trash growth. This would also be true of all other southern Appalachian national forest reservations. By no stretch of the imagination is this an advocacy of anything, most of all the denuding of the public forest lands. The trash removal, however, would leave the woods in far healthier and more attractive condition for renewal of the original forest cover.

During the three and a half decades between 1930 and 1965, the southern states annually retired approximately a million and a half acres of worn out farm lands. Most of this abandoned acreage was left to grow up in self-generated scrub brush and old-field pines. By the latter date, however, the trend of abandoning once cultivated fields was brought largely to a standstill, and by 1977 it had ended completely. Radical changes in the southern agricultural pattern have revolutionized land uses. Cotton as a main staple crop never again approached its primary position after the Great Depression, and by 1950 this crop had largely migrated away from the southern hills to the Southwest and Far West.

During the decades following World War II the Old Southwest made rapid strides in the restoration of its cattle empire, which, historically, dated back to the earliest settlement. The battles against the screw worm and the Texas fever tick were largely won, and pasturage and hay lands quickly supplanted the old row-crop patterns of regional farming. Farm labor had long been in the process of leaving the land, and the war hastened their departure. New demands for pasturage and hay lands brought about the reconversion of areas that in former years would have been turned back to the woods.

Experiment stations in Maryland, Georgia, and Florida were engaged in a worldwide search for hardy grasses that could endure hot dry summers and sustain cattle grazing the year round. Several of the imports proved highly practical and hastened the diversion from cotton and other row crops to pasturage, but the shift was not complete. Plant breeders were meanwhile industriously occupied in developing and improving traditional field crops that could resist devastating insect and disease attacks and triple if not quadruple the old rates of production per acre. This revolution in agriculture, along with the introduction of sophisticated farm machinery and agribusiness procedures, increased production of field crops with only a fraction of the amount of labor required in the past for much smaller harvests.

With the expansion of the new southern industries in the post–World War II South there arose a new breed of part-time farmers who held industrial jobs but at the same time produced more on their modest landholds than did their fathers who devoted full time to farming. Many of these are among the rather large number of forty- and fifty-acre noncorporate private forest owners who came to occupy such a prominent position in southern forestry statistics. As this class of private landowners multiplied, more space was taken up in residential-farmstead sites, community service centers, and pasturage. Between 1965 and 1977 the area of southern forest lands declined from 192 million acres to 188 million. In a more graphic local example, in 1925 Louisiana had 23 million acres of its surface under forest cover, but by 1944 this area had shrunk by 14 million acres. Yet in the decade 1964-1974, wood-using industries invested in that state $640 million in the building and modernizing of paper mills. The state's Forestry Commission reported, however, that there was a greater volume of timber standing in the woods than was being used.

Georgia, the leading pulpwood producing southern state, had an experience comparable to Louisiana's. In the decade following 1961 there was a loss of about a million acres of land to nonforest use. To the south, Florida had lost by 1970 approximately 3.6 million acres of timberlands, leaving 16.7 million acres still in production. The inrush of sun-seeking population and industries and the reversal of the out-flow of people to other parts of the country have all contributed to the reduction of potentially productive timberlands.

In their analysis of the southern timber supply for the future, and in light of the most recent survey of potential growth of softwood stock, Stephen M. Boyce and Herbert A. Knight, of the Southeastern Forest Experiment Station in Asheville, estimated that the growth of softwoods would be increased in the future from an established 2.2 billion cubic feet in 1976 to a projected 7.2 billion by the year 2030. This optimistic prediction presupposes that the same or even a sub-stantially smaller forested area will have to be made to produce more than three times as much wood as at present, and that little or no waste will be left behind by improved harvesting procedures. These analysts expect that a large amount of the new wood will continue to come from noncommercial or privately owned homestead forests, and that this category of forest management will be greatly improved.

If the South meets future challenges for greater wood utilization and production it will have to come to depend heavily upon system-atic regeneration using seedling stock grown from each new stage of genetic improvement, extended periods of growth and lengthened rotations, and more public protection of timberlands from wanton encroachments by nonessential users. Considerable advances in technology and utilization will still have to be made in the removal and consumption of less desirable stock now growing so abundantly in much of the South. It is largely in the latter area that the 40 percent of land now nonproductive will doubtless be brought into full future use. This means that there still lies before the southern forest land-owner and scientists an enormous challenge of applying to timber management a constantly evolving set of advanced principles and industrial procedures. This seems to be a certain fact for the 72 percent of land in the hands of private nonindustrial owners, particularly on the forty-to fifty-acre tracts that currently make up the great body of timberland ownership and management.

As indicated by William R. Haselton of the St. Regis Paper Company, there appear to be bright prospects that southern lands and the wood-using industries, under reasonable conditions, will meet the rising demands of America, and even of much of the world, for wood fiber products. Already headway has been made in this area as indicated by the fact that approximately 12.5 million acres of southern lands had been planted to trees by 1977, and this number is being increased in accelerated proportions each planting season on lands too thinly covered with productive trees, and on clearcut areas. There remain, however, tremendous challenges in the field of man-hastened forest regeneration to assure a rising production of timber up to the staggering volume of wood that will be needed for the next quarter of a century if predictions are correct.

The South does not approach the future in the area of forest management blindly. No other regional economic enterprise in southern history has been so thoroughly surveyed and analysed. With each passing decade more accurate information is accumulated, not only on the present stand, but on the long-range potential. Again whatever may have been the validity of the antebellum boast that "Cotton is King!" that staple commodity never came to occupy so great a position in the national economy as wood products now promise to occupy. The South in 1980 supplied more than two-thirds of the American demand for paper, and both production and demand showed annual increases.

Largely because timber is such a vital renewable resource the Congress of the United States as long ago as 1911 embarked upon a legislative program to safeguard it. In 1974 it enacted the Forest and Rangeland Renewable Natural Resources Planning Act, which opened the way for the making of a searching resources survey to be submitted by the end of December that year and to be updated in 1979 and every decade thereafter. The new legislation in large measure superseded the McSweeney-McNary Act of 1928.

The first and pilot survey was made in South Carolina. This state was chosen because it had such a wide diversity of conditions, ranging from marshy coastal plains and deep alluvial swamps to the Appalachian Highlands. Field work was begun in April 1977 and was completed by September 1978. In time this third national forest survey was extended over the entire South and was, to that date, the most searching and accurate one made of southern forest resources. By 1981 southerners had in hand an impressive body of data from which to shape an accurate profile of their renewable forest, game, land, and water resources.

It is doubtful that many travelers who dash across the South on interstate highways are conscious of the economic significance of the woods through which they pass. Like early nineteenth-century visitors to the region they become bored with the long, monotonous stretches of timberlands. The fate of most of the industrially owned and managed lands through which visitors pass is determined not necessarily by direct human decision, but by the data scientifically trained foresters feed into computers. These machines, tucked away in wood acquisition and land management offices, produce calendars of growth and harvesting times.

It is not difficult to come by reams of statistical information documenting the enormous economic importance of the timber industry to the modern South. As yet no sociologists or economic historians have evaluated its social meaning. In 1972 the value of manufactured products in the South was $2.253 billion, and added to this was another $1.101 billion of supplementary income. Mississippi alone garnered $226 million of the above amount, and even greater portions went to Georgia and Alabama, the two other leading pulpwood producing states. This inflow of capital was reflected in a multiplicity of ways, some obvious, and others so subtle as to be almost indiscernible. For instance, taxable individual incomes increased, and land taxes were stabilized for the first time in southern history. Courthouse-door sales of delinquent lands became a memory.

For appreciable portions of the population in southern timbered areas purchasing power has been increased manyfold since 1935. This is at once noticeable in so superficial an observation as the long Friday checkout lines in chain grocery stores. Where once cotton and tobacco lands only meagerly sustained families and country store ledgers grew bulky with the continuing saga of debtridden customers, cash incomes have closed this chapter of southern history. Once land-poor inheritors of family estates have been restored to affluence partly as a result of their inability to sell lands that were almost worthless in earlier years. Many a modern home, tucked away in suburban pinewoods, has been paid for by the sale of timber, and much of the change in the southern way of life derives from the same source. Less readily visible are the southern bank deposits, which in nine of the most heavily timbered states in 1978 totaled $141.5 billion.

Not so tangible as the full grocery carts, the new homes, or the bank deposits is the element of restored hope in the land for hundreds of thousands of southerners. The old lumber industry opened few if any doors to young southerners to become trained foresters, corporate engineers, land managers, and company executives. Such university-trained specialists now comprise a significant new professional class in southern society, which in places rivals the doctors and lawyers.

But in the turn of southern economic fortunes in this century the acquisition of large blocks of land by state and federal governments, corporations, and by larger private landowners has closed off the path of retreat for many of those forced from the land earlier in this century. Between 1910 and 1935, black and white sharecroppers and tenants, subsistence farmers, and Appalachian highlanders hastened northward up the roads to the eastern seaboard cities and the Great Lakes industrial centers, and to the rising urban and industrial centers of the South. These migrants, black and white, turned their backs on their homeland as virtually dispossesed people. No doubt hundreds of thousands of them dreamed of the day when they could return and take up life where they left off. In the 1980s, however, there is remarkably little land available for the returning natives. In Appalachia they come home to dig out pancake sites on slippery mountainsides to plant trailer homes. These are Harriette Arnow's dollmakers returning to the land with high hopes of inheriting the way of life of their pioneer forebears. Neighboring forests are strewn with their old home places, marked by crumbling chimney piles. Now much of this ancient homeland is enclosed forever by national forests and parks and by corporate holdings. Throngs of John Fox, Jr.'s and Horace Kephart's southern hillmen long ago deserted the regions where these authors found them in the first decades of this century.

A retired pullman car cook came home from New Jersey to resettle his family in South Carolina. He dreamed he would build a modest home and work a garden on the site of his father's tenant shack where he had played and worked as a boy. The land, however, was grown up in pines, and its ownership had passed well beyond his reach. If the forested lands of the South were ever a safety valve for an economically and socially moving urban population they have now ceased to serve that function.

When statisticians speak so empirically of jobs created by the new wood-using industries they fail to reflect the social displacement caused on the land, or the political changes wrought in all phases of the historically "Solid South." That the impersonal corporations will in one way or another exert impressive economic and political power on localities must be assumed as a natural result of so important an investment in the region. It would be unrealistic to imagine a local official, legislator, or governor failing to hear demands made by so vital an agency of resource management, jobs, and capital outlay as the new wood-using corporation. The public and the corporate interests have become such an interwoven fabric that they speak in many parts of the South with a common voice.

The same sun and water that turned much of the South into a magic land also beckon hordes of immigrants to compete for space. This fortunate combination of natural elements, which over untold centuries has nourished the southern forest, now yields a rising flow of wood-based products to comfort pampered Americans, to satisfy their wasteful cravings, and to assure some of them, at least, a future well-being.

For broad sweeps of the South the ancient red-hill badge of shame, so harshly condemned only a half century ago by Big Hugh Bennett, has now been tucked gracefully beneath a blessed tree cover. Along with the vanishing poverty-scored hills have gone the Indian summer haze of perennial forest burnings. Most of the ignorant incendiaries have moved off the land and onto town and city streets to express their angers in other ways; in their place has come a mellower glow to southern sunrises and sunsets.

Once again millions of southern wooded acres have come to have some resemblance to those the old pioneers once trudged with families and herds to hack out humble homesteads and to begin a new way of frontier life. But no longer are there cheap lands, or readily available lands for that matter, and the new forests are never expected to reach the stages of maturity of the old ones.

For the present generation of southerners the land and its managed forest cover can be translated in terms of annual growth, recovery, and capital gains, but of far more enduring importance are the assurances that the South itself is determined to fulfill its obligations to nature, which were set at the beginning of time. Every tree seedling that pushes its head above the rising horizon of the new forest in a sense atones for the shameful errors made by past generations who failed to read clearly the messages of southern nature and land.

The shadow of the future now falls heavily upon the South. For much of the region, history has come full circle. The forerunners of Anglo-American civilization were first seasoned in the forest, and from that date onward the South's economic fortunes remained in large measure anchored in the woods. Prophets of the United States Forest Service in 1981 peered into the future and predicted that the South by 2030 would reduce its wooded acres to 172 million (from 192 in 1952) and private owners would still control two thirds of the timberlands. Corporate owners would show a remarkably small expansion and the Forest Service holdings would show only a negligible gain. In this prediction the South promised not only historical continuity, but to make its forest sufficiently productive to supply consumers wherever they might live on the globe with a growing variety of materials that have come to be considered necessities of modern civilization.

Within the darkening shade of the new Southern forests nature itself is reknitting the disrupted patterns of the past. Deer trails that criss-cross ancient cotton rows beneath the pines reflect the progress of retrieval of the land. The gobbling of wild turkey in distant woods at the first trace of dawn and the barking of squirrels among hard woods hail the restored relationship of wildlife to the southern woods. Of far deeper practical and spiritual meaning is the fact that the human beings who control the fate of the land itself have become far more understanding and responsible and respectful stewards in the management of the South's most substantial heritage, its forests.

Bibliographical Essay

Sources of information about the South's forest resources are almost as numerous and varied as are the region's varieties of trees. Though published materials on particular aspects of the southern woods and the timber industries are not lacking, there is yet no comprehensive general work covering the subject. Regional historians to an amazing degree have neglected the subject in their writings. No southern politician has distinguished himself as a dedicated spokesman for conservation and preservation. Even for the Civilian Conservation Corps and the Tennessee Valley Authority, reforestation was not a matter of central concern. Thus it is difficult to draw together sources on such a diverse subject into a unified bibliography.

There no doubt remain, tucked away in obscure sources that I have not explored, highly pertinent discussions of the South and its forests. No attempt has been made in this bibliography to include any of the numerous technical and specialized scientific materials. Only brief mention is made of the sizable body of state and federal legislation bearing upon the subjects of forestry and conservation.

Since the 1870s various federal agencies have been prolific in making forest surveys and reports. None is of greater basic importance than the decennial censuses and the annual abstracts. The ninth volume of the report of the Tenth Census, 1881, contains an extensive analysis of the then existing national forest resources. This volume is useful for both its statistical data and its fairly eloquent notice of the awakening of government officials to the waste of the forest resources and the approaching exhaustion of the nation's virginal forests. This section of the census report was under the editorship of Charles Sprague Sargent. It was preceded by the important section of the 1875 Report of the Commissioner of Agriculture (Washington, 1876). Remarkably, this report was prepared by personnel of the commissioner's office from such data as were available. Subsequent reports of the commissioner, especially those for 1877, 1911, 1913, and 1933, contain sections on forestry.

For the South specifically Charles Mohr's *The Timber Pine in the Southern United States together with a Discussion of the Structure of their Wood* (Washington, 1897) is a landmark publication, which has been followed by a stream of others on the subject. In the more modern era these include the annual reports and separate publications of the Southern Forest Experiment Station, *A Forest Atlas for the South* (New Orleans, 1969); *A Summary of Timber Resource Review* (Washington, 1958); *An Assessment of the Forest and Range Land Situation in the United States* (Washington, 1980); Stephen G. Boyce and Joe P. McClure, *How to Keep One Third of Georgia in Pines* (Asheville, 1975); Boyce and Herbert A. Knight, *Prospective Ingrowth of Southern Pine beyond 1980* (Asheville, 1979); *Evaluation of Reforestation and Timber Stand Improvement on the National Forest* (Washington, 1978); *Forest Statistics for South Florida 1970* (Asheville, 1970); *Forest Statistics for the United States, 1978* (Washington, 1978); Herbert A. Knight and Joe P. McClure, *Florida's Timber, 1968* (Asheville, 1968); *Land Areas of the National Forest System as of September 30, 1980* (Washington, 1980); Robert W. Larson, *The Timber Supply Outlook in South Carolina* (Washington, 1981); H.C. Leighton and M.R. Hall, *The Relation of the Southern Appalachian Mountains to the Development of Water Power* (Washington, 1908); James P. McCormack, *1946 Commodity Drain by County from South Carolina Forests* (Asheville, 1948); Charles E. McGee and Ralph M. Hooper, *Regeneration after Clearcutting in the Southern Appalachians* (Asheville, 1970); Charles E. McGee, *Regeneration Alternative in Mixed Oaks* (Asheville, 1975); and *Regeneration Trends 10 Years after Clearcutting of an Appalachian Hardwood Stand* (Forest Service Research Note Se-227, Asheville, December 1975); *Multiresource Inventories—A New Concept for Forest Survey* (Asheville, 1979); Paul A. Murphy, *Louisiana Forester: Status and Outlook* (New Orleans, 1975); *Pine Reforestation Task Force Report for Southern Forests* (n.p., ca. June 1977).

A summary view of forest development in the South is contained in *The Bluebook of Southern Progress* (Baltimore, 1927-1941), a publication of the *Manufacturers Record*. A comprehensive statistical source is *Southern Pulpwood Production*, issued annually (Asheville, 1960-1980), by various forest statisticians.

Of an earlier vintage are the voluminous reports of the United States Bureau of Soils. These contain a vast amount of physical, sociological, and historical data pertinent to an understanding of forest growth. Cited here specifically is Part I, numbers 1-14 (Washington, 1923). These contain data on North and South Carolina, Georgia, Florida, Mississippi, and Texas.

Individual research and special publications are: Raymond M. Sheffield, *Forest Statistics for South Carolina, 1978* (Asheville, 1979); R. R. Reynolds, *The Crossett Story: The Beginnings of Forestry in Southern Arkansas and Northern Arkansas* (New Orleans, 1979); *The Forest Situation in the United States, A Special Report to the Timber Board, Jan. 30, 1932* (Washington, June 1977); *The South's Third Forest. A Southern Forest Resources Analysis* (n.d., n. p.); *Timber Resources for America's Future*, Forest Resources Report 14 (Washington, n. d.); *Trends in Commercial Timberland Areas in the United States by State and Ownership, 1959-1977: Projections to 2030* (Washington, 1981); Philip C. Wakeley, *Planting the*

Southern Pine, Agricultural Monograph No. 18 (Washington, 1954); Richard L. Welch and Thomas R. Bellamy, *Changes in Output of Industrial Products in Florida, 1969-1975* (Asheville, 1977).

State Forestry Publications

Since 1920 all the southern states have created departments of forestry, and all of them have published reports and other materials. Among these publications are the annual reports of the South Carolina Forestry Commission (Columbia, 1961-1975); A. Keith and C.C. Goodwin, *North Carolina History Series,* vol. I, no. 3 (Raleigh, 1969); Thomas W. Birch and Douglas S. Powell, *The Forest Land Owners of Kentucky,* Forest Resource Bulletin NE-57 (Broomell, Pennsylvania, 1976); Paul Camplin, ed., *Forestry in Kentucky* (Frankfort, 1966); Lafayette DeFries, *Report on a Belt of Kentucky Timbers East and West along the South Central Part of the State from Columbus to Pound Gap,* Report of Special Subjects, Geological Survey of Kentucky, new series (Frankfort, 1884); Jacqueline M. Earles, *Statistics for Louisiana Parishes* (New Orleans, 1975); *Forestry in Mississippi: Its Economic Impact* (Jackson, 1976); *The Golden Dawn of Louisiana's Third Forest* (Alexandria, 1974); Neal P. Kingsley and Douglas S. Powell, *The Forest Resources of Kentucky* (Frankfort, 1977); Lawrence J. Dewel and Frank O. Lege, *Availability of Timber on Lands of Farm and Miscellaneous Owners in Florida* (n.d., n.p.); *Louisiana Forest Types* (Baton Rouge, n.d.), which contains a map indicating the location of various types of trees; Richard L. Porterfield, Thomas R. Terfehr, and James E. Mook, *Forestry and the Mississippi Economy* (Starkville, 1978); *Plant Trees in Kentucky, a Multiple Benefit Activity* (Frankfort, 1976); *Second Report of the Kentucky Agricultural Society to the Legislature of Kentucky, 1858-1859* (Frankfort, 1860); Walton R. Smith and Jerry D. McCord, *Harvesting Florida's Forest, Yesterday, Today, and Tomorrow* (Tallahassee, 1977); *Timber and Pulpwood Production in Louisiana* (Baton Rouge, 1978); Annual Reports of the Arkansas Forestry Commission (Little Rock, 1934-1944); A.S. Todd and R.R. Craig, *Forest Resources of the Coastal Plain of South Carolina* (Columbia, 1948); *Wood Using Industries of Louisiana,* Louisiana Forestry Commission Bulletin 6 (Baton Rouge, 1976).

Manuscript Collections

The records of the Burt-Brabb Lumber Company, Ford, Kentucky, 1890-1912, in the Samuel M. Wilson Collection, Margaret I. King Library, University of Kentucky, are excellent. A personal insight into pioneer forestry training in the South is to be found in the correspondence of William E. Jackson. A student of Carl A. Schenck, Jackson visited Germany from October 1909 to April 1910. These letters are in the possession of his daughters, Susan Jackson Keig of Chicago and Billy Jackson Bower of Lexington, Kentucky.

Several major periodicals have devoted generous space to southern forestry and conservation, publicizing the activities of George Vanderbilt, Gifford Pinchot, and Carl Alwin Schenck and the crusades to check forest fires, to organize departments of forestry, and to better utilize wood products. Useful material appears in the national journals of forestry and in that voluminous chronicle of southern economics, *The Manufacturers Record, a Weekly Southern Industries, Railroad, and Financial Newspaper* (Baltimore, 1881-). The selected articles listed here are grouped under the periodicals in which they appeared.

A leader among the forestry journals for nearly a century has been the journal of the American Forestry Association, published under various titles: *The Forester*, 1895-1901; *Forestry and Irrigation*, 1902-1908; *Conservation*, 1908-1909; *American Forestry*, 1910-1923; *American Forest and Forest Life*, 1910-1923; *American Forests*, 1931- . Since its founding in 1895, the volumes of this journal have been numbered consecutively without regard to the title changes. Articles of interest include: J.B. Atkinson, "Planting Forests in Kentucky," 16 (August 1910): 449-53; Stuart Campbell, "The Land Problem in Florida," 40 (January 1934): 26-27; James G. Needham, "Between Hills and the Sea," 39 (May 1933): 198; "South Carolina Needs a Forestry Department," 30 (September 1924): 614-15; George Vanderbilt, "Pioneer in Forestry," 20 (June 1914): 421.

The Forest Farmer: Phillip R. Wheeler, "Report of the Southern Forest Analysis, A Summary," 28 (July 1960): 6-9.

The Journal of Forest History: Anna C. Burns, "Henry E. Hardtner, Louisiana's First Conservationist," 22 (April 1978): 78-85; Thomas D. Clark, "Kentucky Logmen," 25 (July 1981): 144-57; James E. Fickle, "Defense Mobilization in the Southern Pine Industry: The Experience of World War I," 22 (October 1978): 206-23; Gerry Reed, "Saving the Naval Stores Industry: Charles Holmes Herty's Cup and Gutter Experiment, 1900-1908," 26 (October 1982): 168-75; Jerold Shofner, "Forced Labor in the Florida Forests, 1880-1950," 25 (January 1981): 14-25.

The Journal of Forestry: Raiford F. Brown, "Forestry in the Soil Conservation Program in Northern Mississippi," 39 (July 1941): 598-600; Austin Gary, "Some Relations of Fire to Longleaf Pine," 43 (May 1945): 595, 601; Darrow W. Clark, "The Problem of Development of the North Carolina Forest Organization," 31 (November 1933): 742-49, "Forest Schools in the United States," 17 (November 1919): 673-80, 696; "The Longleaf Pine," 14 (September 1916): 513-20; J. E. Barton, "Initiating a State Forest Policy in Kentucky," 18 (January 1914): 135-41; "Franklin B. Hough: A Tribute," 19 (July 1921): 431-32; J.S. Ilick, "The Pines of the South," 19 (August 1921): 551-59; "The Case of the State of Louisiana," 17 (July 1911): 414-23; R.D. Garner, "The Portable Sawmill and Selective Loggers in Second Growth Loblolly Pine," 39 (January 1941): 971-

76; Richard Kilbourne, "Watershed Improvements in the Tennessee Valley," 58 (April 1960), 295-96; G.H. Lentz, D. Sinclair, and H.G. McGinnis, "Soil Erosion in the Silt Loam Upland of Mississippi," 28 (November 1930): 971-76; W.R. Mattoon, "William Willard Ashe, 1872-1932," 30 (May 1932): 652-53, 906-07; Lloyd E. Smith, "Development of Second Growth Pine in Southern Mississippi," 53 (September 1953): 648-49; "South Leads Nation in Pulpwood Production," 50 (January 1952): 39; Carl Williams, "The Land Use Problems in the South," 28 (May 1932): 276-83; S.R. Young, "The Role of Forest Products in Railroad Revenue," 30 (May 1932): 318-22; E.A. Ziegler and W.E. Bond, "Financial Aspects of Growing Pines in the South," 30 (March 1932): 284-97.

The Manufacturers Record: Stanley G. Arthur, "Reforestation as a Solution of the South's Cut-over Land Problem," 72 (26 July 1917): 66b-66c; "Big Pulp Mill for Wilmington," 72 (27 August 1917): 61; "Bowaters Dedicates Tennessee Plant," 122 (11 November 1954): 28, 55; Charles Chidsey, "Naval Stores in the South," 43 (1 May 1913): 63; "Forty-Five Vessels Underway of Those Contracted for at Pascagoula," 73 (10 January 1918): 55-56; "General Goethals Invited South to see Wooden Ship Building Conditions," 71 (7 June 1917): 80; Frank C. Gilreath, "Investigating Opportunities in Georgia and Alabama for the Manufacture of High Grade Paper from Slash Pine," 99 (5 June 1930): 63; "Great Shipbuilding and Lumber Operations," 72 (12 July 1917): 55; Henry S. Graves, "Lumber Industry and Conservation," 65 (14 May 1914): 48-49); "Large Plywood Factory at Macon Backed by Russian and English Capital," 71 (11 January 1917): 52; "Launching of First Wooden Ship Built at Houston, Texas, the Nacogdoches," 73 (18 April 1918): 61-62; "Letters from Southern Lumbermen on Reasons Why Government's Wooden Ship Building Has Been Delayed," 73 (14 March 1918): 61-62; "Lumber Production in 1929," 99 (14 May 1931): 32; Don McCleland, "Pensacola and Vicinity Show Notable Growth in Shipbuilding Activity," 73 (10 January 1918): 63-64; "Making Paper in Mississippi," 63 (5 June 1913): 67-68; Hu Maxwell, "Timber Resources in the South," 63 (27 March 1913): 41-42; "Mississippi Paper Mill Working Twenty-four Hours a Day," 67 (6 March 1915): 49; "Mobile to Become Great Shipbuilding Center," 73 (10 January 1918): 64; "More Than $164,000,000 Worth of Ships Under Contract and Being Built in Four Southeastern States," 73 (10 January 1918): 61-62; "New Source of Wealth in South's Pine Forests," 101 (7 July 1932): 13-14; "Opportunities for Shipbuilding at Appalachicola, Florida," 73 (3 January 1918): 81-82; "Over $4,000,000 for Steel and Wooden Ships Now Building in the South," 99 (5 June 1930): 28-29; Albert Phenix, "Southern Appalachian Forest Resume," 65 (25 June 1914): 41-43; "Pulpwood for Paper," 65 (17 March 1914): 52; "Research Pulp and Paper Plant Underway," 101 (17 March 1932): 25-26; "Ship Timber in Abundance Available in the South," 71 (31 May 1917): 51-52; "South's Ability to Supply Abundance of Lumber for Ships Completely Demonstrated," 71 (7 June 1917): 51-53; "South as Nation's Greatest Source of Pulpwood," 97 (20 March 1930): 42; "Southward the Paper-Making Industry moves," 97 (13 March 1930): 56; W.P. Sullivan, "Complete Utilization of Waste by World's Largest Sawmill," 72 (5 July 1917): 80; "To Vitalize 100,000 Acres of Cut-Over Lands in the South for Agriculture," 71 (19 April 1917): 57-58; E.P. Veitch and J.L. Merrill, "Pulp and Paper and Other Products from Waste Resinous Woods," 63 (13 March 1913): 53; "Virginia's Place in Forestry," 65 (28 February 1914): 53; "Vigorous Protest by Southern Lumbermen Against Charges of Failure to Furnish Ship Timbers as Required," 73 (7 March 1918): 79-80; C.A. Whittle, "South as a Source of Wood Pulp," 97 (26 March 1930): 46; C.P. Winslow, "Pulp and Papers from Southern Woods," 101 (24 March 1931): 20-23; "Wooden Ships Program Not to be Abandoned," 71 (31 May 1917): 50.

In its Christmas 1956 issue, the *Southern Lumberman*, Nashville, celebrated its 75th anniversary in the concluding section of volume 193. In this 370-page number the periodical made a broad survey of both southern forestry and lumbering history. The more pertinent articles are: Ed Kerr, "From Timber to Famine and Back Again," 139-43; Philip R. Wheeler and Herbert Sternitzke, "Timber Trends in the Mid-South," 179-81; Richard E. McArdle, "Seventy-Five Years in Southern Forestry," 119-21; Elwood Maunder, "The *Southern Lumberman* and American History," 124-26; M.L. Fleishel, "The First Forty-Two Years," 173-76; Victor B. McNaughton, "Something of Value," 187-88; H.J. Malsberger, "Seventy-Five Years History of Wood Pulp and Paper Industry in the South," 182-84. Articles relating to specific states are: Hilton Watson, "Alabama's Sawmill Industry," 158-61; George S. Brewer, "Timber, Arkansas' Leading Resource," 152-56; Douglas C. Brookshire, "Carolina's Lumber Industry," 161-62; William Gaber, "Lumbering in Florida," 164-66; Joseph Kovach, "The Lumber Industry in Georgia," 156-58; Burdine Webb, "Old Times in Eastern Kentucky," 178g-178j; Nollie Hickman, "Mississippi Lumber Industry, 1840-1950," 132-37; Paul B. Kramer, "The Texas Story," 178c-178g.

The Appalachian Forestry Crusade

The so-called Appalachian Crusade, which marked a turning point in the conservation of regional natural resources, and the struggle to bring about the passage of the Weeks Law generated a considerable volume of writings.

Among articles appearing in *Conservation* and *American Forestry* (both predecessors to *American Forests*, as explained above) were: W.W. Ashe, "Practicality of State Forests in Southern Appalachian States," 15 (May 1909): 275-82; "The Fight for the Appalachian Forests," ibid. 251; George F. Smith, "The Equalizing Influence of Forests on the Flow of Streams and Their Value as a Means of Improving Navigation," ibid. (August 1909) 489-94; John H. Finney, "The South's Concern in the Appalachian Project and How to Make

Its Influence Felt," ibid. (December 1909): 741-51; "The Passage of the Appalachian Bill," 17 (February 1911): 164-67; "The Appalachian Bill," ibid. 168-70; Thomas Nelson Page, "The People's Possessions in the Appalachian Forest," ibid. (March 1911): 133-44; "The Appalachian Forests," ibid. (July 1911): 381-83; W.W. Hall, "The Appalachian Work," 18 (March 1912): 192; Louis S. Murphy, "The Weeks Law Collaborators Conference," 19 (February 1913): 113-17; "Purchase of Appalachian Forest," ibid. (March 1913): 193; Raymond Pullman, "Destroying Mt. Mitchell," 21 (February 1915): 83-93; "American Appalachian Purchase," 22 (October 1916): 611; R.O.E. Davis, "Erosion in the Appalachian Piedmont region," 25 (September 1919): 135-36

Tracing the Weeks Bill through the confusing maze of Congressional references becomes an exercise in frustration. The bill first appears in the *Congressional Record* as H.B. 26922, January 22, 1909 (43 [2]: 1924); it was reintroduced March 26, 1920, as H.B. 23633 (45 [4]: 3835). The engrossed bill, as finally enacted March 1, 1911, is in *United States Statues at Large* 36 (1):961. The administration and workings of the Weeks Law and its subsequent amendments are revealed in the reports of the National Forest Reservation Commission (Washington, 1913-1980).

State and Agricultural
Historical Quarterlies

Reuben Robertson, "Recent Developments in Southern Forestry," *Georgia Review* 5 (Fall 1951): 362-68; Paul F. Sharp, "The Tree Farm Movement: Its Origin and Development," *Agricultural History* 23 (January 1949): 41-45; J.M. Stauffer, "Forestry in Alabama," *Alabama History Quarterly*, 10: 65-67.

Federal Forestry Agency Reports
and Special Articles

Two federal agencies have played roles in the development of southern reforestation. Both gave a tremendous boost to the region during the Great Depression and the era of exhaustion of the "first forest."

The most informative sources for the Civilian Conservation Corps program are Robert Fechner's annual reports and other official writings, 1933-1941. Considerable attention was devoted to the early work of the CCC in the journal *American Forests*: John Thompson Auten, "The Story of 'Hay Holler,'" 39 (September 1933): 387-89; "CCC Records Accomplishments," 40 (February 1934): 40, 82; "The Emergency Conservation Project," 39 (July 1933): 309; Gus Lentz, "Making Water Walk in the Tennessee Valley," 40 (May 1934): 200-201; R.S. Maddox, "Reclaiming Tennessee Lands. How Reforestation can Contribute to the Reconstruction of Eroded Soils in the Tennessee Valley," 39 (April 1933): 148-50; "March Heads CCC Education," 40 (February 1934): 80-

81; "Start Erosion Control Work in Tennessee Valley," 39 (December 1933): 562. "The Forestry Corps in Review," 39 (August 1933): 497; R.Y. Stuart, "That 250,000 Man Job," 39 (May 1933): 195-97, "With the Civilian Conservation Corps," 39 (July 1933): 302.

Historically significant is the fact that the years of the CCC coincided with the beginnings of the Tennessee Valley Authority. The Corps contributed substantially to the success of the TVA forestry and land conservation programs. Sources on the latter agency, in addition to the agency's annual reports, are: *A Short History of the Tennessee Valley Authority, 40th Anniversary of People in Partnership* (Knoxville, 1973), "A Suggestion for Legislation to Congress to Create the Tennessee Valley Authority," *The Public Papers and Addresses of Franklin D. Roosevelt* (New York, 1938) 2: 122-29; James Dahir, *Region Building, Community Development Lessons from the Tennessee Valley* (New York, 1955); John W. Hershey, "Tree Crops for Tennessee Valley Farms," *American Forests* 40 (October 1934): 474-75, 502; B.W. Jones, "The Valley of Lost Hope," ibid. (July 1934): 298-300; Edward C.M. Richards, "The Role of Forests in the Tennessee Valley," ibid. 40 (October 1934): 471-73, 500; David Lilienthal, *TVA: Democracy on the March* (New York, 1944); C.H. Pritchett, *The Tennessee Valley Authority, a Study in Public Administration* (Chapel Hill, 1943); Frank Smith, *Land Between the Lakes, Experiment in Recreation* (Lexington, 1971); *TVA Today* (special issue) May 1973; J.S. Ransmeier, *T.V.A. Case Study in the Economics of Multiple Purpose Stream Planning* (Nashville, 1942).

Corporate Sources

Most of the modern wood-using companies in the South have published reports and other materials concerning their operations and landholdings. Least responsive to requests for information was the International Paper Corporation. Sources consulted include the annual reports of Mead Corporation, Champion International Corporation, Union-Camp, and Weyerhaeuser Corporation; the quarterly publication *Reach* published by St. Regis; and *Champion Magazine*. Also: *A History of Mead* (Dayton, 1981): Eleanor Amigo and Mark Neuffer, *Beyond the Adirondacks, The Story of the St. Regis Paper Company* (West, Conn., 1980); *Bowater in Catawba* (Catawba, S.C., n.d.); *Mead Financial Fact Book* (Dayton, 1981); *Weyerhaeuser Handy Facts* (n.p., 1981); George H. Weyerhaeuser, *Forests for the Future, The Weyerhaeuser Story* (New York, 1981); Jonathan Daniels, *The Forest is the Future* (New York: International Paper, 1957).

Regional Newspapers

The southern newspaper press, 1880 to date, has shown an active interest in the utilization of the region's forest resources. I consulted many of these papers, among them *The State* (Columbia, S. C.), *Atlanta Constitution and Journal*, *News and Observer* (Raleigh, N. C.), *Clarion Ledger* (Jackson, Miss.), *Nashville Banner*, *Louisville Courier-Journal*, *Augusta* (Ga.) *Chronicle*, *Charlotte Observer*. These papers have carried frequent news stories about forest industries, and their managers were actively interested in the Herty newsprint venture.

General Works

Though an appreciable volume of published material relates to the southern timber industry, few books have dealt specifically with the subject. Among those relating to the subject are: G. Norman Bishop, *Native Trees of Georgia* (Athens, 1959); Pete Daniels, *The Shadow of Slavery: Peonage in the South, 1901-1969* (Urbana, 1972); Lucy E. Braun, *Deciduous Forests of Western North America* (Philadelphia, 1950); Herman B. Chapman, *Forest Management* (Albany, 1931); Robert B. Collins, *A History of the Daniel Boone National Forest, 1770-1970* (Lexington, 1975); William Duerr, *The Economic Problem of Forestry in the Appalachian Region* (Cambridge, 1949); James E. Fickle, *The New South and "The New Competition": Trade Association Development in the Southern Pine Industry* (Urbana, 1980); A.H. Harrison, Jr., *How to Get Rich in the South* (Chicago, 1888); Nollie Hickman, *Mississippi Harvest, Lumbering in the Longleaf Pine Belt, 1840-1915* (University, Mississippi, 1962); Calvin B. Hoover and Ben U. Ratchford, *Economic Resources and Policies of the South* (New York, 1951); *Manual Edition of the Forest Farmer* (Atlanta, 1966); Roscoe C. Martin, *From Forest to Front Page* (University, Alabama, 1956); Elwood Maunder, interviewer, *Voices from the South, Recollections of Four Foresters* (Santa Cruz, 1977); Almon E. Parkins, *The South, Its Economic-Geographic Development* (New York, 1938); Howard W. Odum, *Southern Regions of the United States* (Chapel Hill, 1936); Harold T. Pinkett, *Gifford Pinchot, Private and Public Forester* (Urbana, 1970); Arthur F. Raper, *Tenants of the Almighty* (New York, 1943); Carl Alwin Schenck, *The Birth of Forestry in America: Biltmore Forest School 1898-1913* (Santa Cruz, 1974); Mary Verhoeff, *Kentucky River Navigation* (Louisville, 1917); Mary Wharton and Roger Barbour, *Trees and Shrubs of Kentucky*, (Lexington, 1975); Ralph B. Widener, *Forests and Foresters in the United States, a Reference Anthology*, (Washington, 1950); Robert K. Winters, ed., *Fifty Years of Forestry in the U.S.A.*, (Washington, 1950).

Directories and Encyclopedias

The Dictionary of Paper including Pulp, Paperboard Properties, and Related Paper-Making Terms (New York, 1965); *Encyclopedia of American Forest and Conservation History*, 2 vols., (New York, 1983); *Lockwood's Directory of the Pulp and Paper Mills in the United States* (New York, 1976).

Index

Head, F.H., 16
Hershey, John W., 88
Herty, Charles Holmes, 23, 46, 104-05, 106-08, 110, 112, 114, 118, 129, 137
Herty cup, 46, 104
Hiwassee Land Company, 96
Hiwassee River, 92, 93, 96
Holman, Jack, 48
Holmes, Joseph Austin, 44-45, 47
homesteading, 15-16
Hough, Franklin Benjamin, 37-38, 39
Houlton Lumber Company, 31
Houston, Texas, 30; shipyard, 28
Howland, Paul, 60
How to Get Rich in the South, 14
Hull, Cordell, 61
Huntsville, Alabama, 92
Hyde, Joseph H., 48

Illinois, 16, 98
Illinois Central Railroad, 30, 31
Indiana, 16
Indianapolis, Indiana, 35
Indians, 2, 3, 4, 5, 12, 35; reservations, 58
Indian territories, 1, 65
Interior, U.S. Department of the, 75; secretary, 61; Soil Erosion Service, 78
International Paper Company, 105, 108, 119-20
Interstate Investment Company, 45

Jackson, William E., 43
Jackson (Mississippi) *Clarion-Ledger*, 121
Jackson Purchase, 100
Jacksonville, Florida, 28, 29
Jasper County, Texas, 118, 125
J.E. Sirrine Company, 93
Josephson, H.R. 95
Journal of American Forestry, 68
Junction, Florida, 50

Kansas, 16
Kellogg, R.S., 56
Kemper County, Mississippi, 121
Kennedy, John F., 99
Kentucky, 11, 24, 59, 61, 99, 100, 123, 140; coal, 98, 99; Commissioner of Agriculture, 7; eastern, 45, 62, 63, 98; General Assembly, 99; lumber harvests, 24; rafting, 24

Kentucky Dam, 99
Kentucky, University of, 24
Kentucky River: North Fork, 24
Kephart, Horace, 12-13, 145
Kidder, Edward, 10
Kilsock Bay, 120
Kingsport, Tennessee, 123, 124
Knight, Herbert A., 142
Knoxville, Tennessee, 93
Knoxville News-Sentinel, 96

Labor, U.S. Department of, 75
labor peonage, 22-23, 34
Lamar, Alabama, 121
Land Between the Lakes, 99-100
land costs and sales, 15, 16, 45
Landsat II, 125
land use programs, 51, 62, 65, 80, 138
Latins, 5
Laurel, Mississippi, 27
Lawrenceburg, Kentucky, 43
Lee, Florida, 125
Lever, Asbury Francis, 61
Lilienthal, David, 89, 93, 101
Lloyd George, David, 26
loaders, 136
loblolly pine (*pinus taeda*), 3-4, 31, 51, 57, 91, 103-04, 109, 114; extent, 15; growing conditions, 9, 10; in paper industry, 118, 121, 122
London, England, 92
longleaf pine (*pinus palustris*), 2-3, 4, 15, 25, 120; depletion, 30; extent, 15, 17, 103, 106; growing conditions, 9, 54-55; uses, 2-3
Longstreet, A.B., 12
Lookout Mountain, battle of, 52
Louisiana, 55, 56, 68, 114; Forestry Commission, 142; General Assembly, 55, 56; Land Office and Commission of Forestry, 56; land purchases, 16; paper mills, 125; pine forests, 15, 69, 72; St. Bernard Parish, 38
Louisiana Fibre Board Company, 33
Louisville, Kentucky, 45
Louisville and Nashville Railroad, 18
Lowndes County, Mississippi, 122
Lowville, New York, 37
Lufkin, Texas, 108
lumber industry, 8, 13, 18-19, 30, 69-72;